SZAROTKA

Adam J. Galanski-De León

American Buffalo Books
Manhattan, KS

American Buffalo Books
www.AmericanBuffaloBooks.org

The Library of Congress has cataloged
the American Buffalo Books paperback as follows:
Names: Galanski-De León, Adam J, author
Title: Szarotka: a novel / Adam J. Galanski-De León
Description: Manhattan, KS: American Buffalo Books, 2024
Library of Congress Control Number: 2024943478
ISBN: 9798218483067

Printed in the United States of America
1st printing

Cover design: Jordan Stegeman
Author photo: Kyle Eddy

"Death-glorious ship!
Must ye then perish, and without me?"
— Herman Melville

You dedicate this book to your mother.

ROBOTNIK

September is a horny old man hustling the street corner at dusk. He rolls his busted wheelchair around the curve of the sidewalk and shouts to passing couples as the bus lurches by, "You're a lucky guy! Christ, she's beautiful." The sky is orange and black. The high-rises are a defeated gray. The old man's heart is blue as he confides in another hustler, "I'm gonna get some. I'm gonna get some tonight." And the other hustler spots the drought behind his eagerness and knows it not to be true.

You get on that bus heading east to Goose Island, watching the man wheel away headed west, and crane your neck back after him, while the city slides by the window like the repeating background of a vintage cartoon.

The bus passes over the Chicago River on the rusted iron bridge composed of trusses, and the last gasp of the blazing sun reflects its scream in the glass of the distant skyscrapers. A barge sulks in the waters below. Gulls whistle and screech. Geese flap away from the manmade bend in the industrial river, formed like a check mark in an unbalanced V.

* * *

Fall is the light of the factory, bleeding into the empty streets, rustling with burning leaves in the wind that smells of gasoline.

* * *

"Why do you want to work in manufacturing?" your interviewer asks. He wears a red and blue checkered shirt buttoned to the top of the collar. His brown hair was combed neat earlier but is now ruffled.

His face reveals the question is merely protocol. He is uninterested in your answer.

"I'm sick of customer service," you tell him. "I just want to work."

* * *

At 9 a.m., you ride the 56 bus an hour north to the Six Corners at Irving Park. It is the earliest you have woken up on purpose in years. A man with a busted left eye, crusted with dried blood, lights up a cheap cigar. His skin is ashen, fingers caked with dirt. His beard is a faded black and gray. His clothes are ripped and tattered, smeared with stains from sleeping on the street.

"I know, I know," he says in response to that look you are giving him. The windows of the bus are fogged. You are choking behind your face mask. The bus reaches Irving Park, and you stand to get up. "I told you I'd get you," he sneers. You are unsure if he is talking to you, but he looks in your eyes with pure animosity and points a crooked finger in your face. "I told you I'd get you, bitch."

"You're gonna die alone in the gutter. And I'll piss on your fucking grave. Nobody but the coroner will know you ever lived," you wish to say. You return his malicious stare and exit the bus.

Hatred is the language of the ignored or the overly adored relinquished of their accolades. The streets of the city rage like a beaten drum. The eyes of the hopeless lurk the corner pawn shop, nursing rotten track marks and Styrofoam cups of change.

* * *

The company has paid for your physical at a hole-in-the-wall doctor's office on the Six Corners. The secretary asks that you please take a seat. You wait in the empty room for 45 minutes, watching *Maury* with subtitles before a nurse calls you back. You never find out who is the father of the child.

The first examination room is cramped and smells of disinfectant. The nurse is a young woman. She has green eyes, is a natural blond, slim, and athletic. Three diamond studs line each of her earlobes. A more illustrious diamond sparkles in the office light on a band around her left ring finger. Her skin is healthy and flawless. It makes you conscious of your face, riddled with pock marks and minor scars, your smile missing a tooth from past altercations.

"Pee in this cup for me," she says, marking two lines with a Sharpie on the side of the plastic. "Make sure you fill it between these two measures." You take the cup from her hands and examine it, wondering if you'll be able to squeeze out any urine, not having drank anything today.

"Do I have to piss in front of you?" You ignore her eye roll because it was a legitimate question.

"Go in that bathroom."

"Can I close the door?"

"Sure."

When she receives your warm cup of bronze piss, she leads you to another examination room where you are asked 40 rounds of yes-or-no questions regarding your medical history. "Are you on any narcotic medications?" she asks.

Unsure what that means, you say, "Is risperidone a narcotic?" Her face shows your ignorance has offended her.

"What's risperidone?"

"An anti-psychotic."

"Then you're probably fine."

She hands you a pale floral gown and asks that you change into it before the doctor arrives. You will be receiving some x-rays momentarily. You put it on but have trouble tying the back and ultimately give up, exposing your ass to the stale sheet paper on the examination bed. This decision proves to be poor when the doctor introduces herself and asks that you follow her down the office hallway. Halfway down the hall, a sympathetic nurse stops you and ties the strings tight. After the x-rays, the doctor instructs you to put your forearms on the table, lying flat.

She attaches sticker sensors across your palms and fingers before attaching an electronic machine with a chip. Before you can ask what these are for, she is sending electric shocks through your hands. Your nerves jolt in sharp pain as the shocks pulse, first in spurts and then steady as a metronome. Your fingers curl back mechanically with each pulse. They look like the gnarled ends of tree branches, barren of leaves. When the pain becomes too much to bear and your motivation to work in the factory begins to wane, the doctor removes the stickers and brings you to a door down the hallway.

Here she has a milk crate filled with 50 pounds of weight. She asks you to pick it up properly and bend it back to the floor five times for her. This task would be simpler if your wrists had not just been zapped with electricity to the point of physical trauma. As you drop the weights back to the floor, bending your knees, the tip of your manhood slips out the bottom of the pastel gown, which was already too short to begin with. The doctor gives an endearing smile and sends you on your way.

* * *

It is Monday morning, and you walk down the street of boutiques and upscale bars choking out the Old Style signs and dilapidated Polish restaurants of a bygone Chicago. The blue stringed lights in the shedding trees at the triangle on Milwaukee and Division are still lit from the nighttime. Leaves blanket the waterless fountain and red cobblestones below, contrasting with the torn shoes of smoking vagrants in a somber mosaic.

Swings creak back and forth in the wind on the playground of Holy Trinity High School. "Kościół Trójcy Świętej," reads the sign above the entrance of the Holy Trinity Church next door. "Polska Szkoła," reads another on the side of the building. Your lips fumble trying to pronounce these words. A portrait of a white Jesus is plastered up above the highway with the caption "JESUS I TRUST IN YOU" for all the passing drivers to recite in their minds.

You make your way through the Kennedy Expressway underpass. The tents and desolate mattresses of the unhoused are empty and strewn with broken glass and trash. The sun is rising through the trusses of the iron bridge, highlighting the umber rust with an overbearing orange, which blinds you. The geese violently honk everywhere from the beams to the barges to the pillars jutting out of the water.

One hisses at you like a bobcat, its black tongue quivering with its wings outstretched. You put up your fists in defense like you would actually box a bird. It waddles away, pattering its equally black webbed feet on the chipped concrete. On North Branch, you turn to see the street sweepers gassing up at the city worker fuel station next to the police drinking coffee in militant SUV's, cracking half-witted jokes about life going on another day.

* * *

"Listen up because I'm only gonna explain this once. From these boxes over here, you grab a ball valve, T-piece, two union nuts, two union tailpieces, a long nip, a short nip, an elbow, and an adapter nut. Smear sealant around the plumber's tape on the threads of a tailpiece. They tape these things like shit so you might have to re-tape it yourself. Put a nut around it backwards and screw the tailpiece on to this end of the valve ball. Apply sealant to this end of the T-piece and attach it to the other end of the valve ball. Then take the other tailpiece with the nut around it facing this way, add sealant, and turn it on the open end of the T-piece. Now throw those two brass rings on each side and stick it on that piece in the vise. Take this big-ass Torx wrench and turn the top till the tape is gone. You might need to use the adjustable wrench on those flat-bottom divots to hold the ball valve still while you do this. When both ends are tight, buff the gunk out with a rag. Take this pokey thing and rip out the excess tape. Kinda like a dentist uses to count teeth, huh? Then put sealant on both ends of the short nip, screw it in the hole on the T-piece, attach the elbow, the long nip, and the nut adapter. Wrench the short nip tight and take this impact wrench and fit it around the nut adapter and pull the trigger till the plumbing tape is gone. Careful, it's loud, and you'll get shit in your eyes. Wear glasses and ear plugs, OSHA standards. Then buff the shit out of that with the rag again and scratch excess tape off with the dental tool. Take this bubble level and make sure the long nip is balanced, then take this puzzle-piece-looking thing and hold it up to both sides, making sure you've wrenched it enough to fit in correctly. Now unscrew those gold rings with your hands, and you got yourself a valve! Got it? Now put that on the rack and do it again for the next eight hours."

Your supervisor leaves you at your station to absorb everything he just told you. Some of his instructions were lost behind the blasting of drills and other machinery. After a few failed attempts, you take the example he assembled and do your best to make your valve imitate that. At 3:30 p.m., you have made 36 valves. The rack is carted away for testing. Only two valves show signs of leakage. You will fix them the next day before filling another rack.

* * *

Redemption is the gloss in your mother's eye. She bats a lash, and a tear rolls down.

"I got that job," you tell her, "I'll send you something from each paycheck as they come."

"Bless you, serduszko," she tells you. "Your father would be proud."

She rests her hand atop yours on the dining room table. Green spider veins stretch above her pale bones like glacial rivers, roadmaps to her heart.

"Where did I go wrong?" she now asks. It stings. It stings because you know it wasn't her.

It was you.

"Where did I go wrong to make you suffer so? Was it your papa? Was it me? Did I not show you enough love?"

"You're the only one who showed me love," you tell her. Now your eyes are glossy too.

"Promise me, you keep this job," your mother tells you. "This is new path for you. This is straight and narrow!"

"I will, Mama," you tell her. "I'll try."

* * *

Repetition is the water of the lake consuming the shoreline. You are a tooth in the jaws of industry, consuming the flesh of the American landscape. Unconsciousness is as much a part of your lifestyle as is the need to stare down the sunset on 31st Street Beach after a shift that taught you the meaning of eternity.

The first 36 valves you made have now spanned into the hundreds, but the owner of the factory has expressed distrust in you to your supervisor. He thinks you are too slow. You now must fill a sheet out with your start and stop times throughout the day, marking how many valves of each type you have completed. Staring at the physical numbers of your work ignites a sense of dignity within your profession. You grow uneasy as the tally marks unfold over the weeks and never end.

* * *

On your way to the break room for lunch, you stop in the men's room to wash off the gunk that has accumulated on your torn-up fingers. You bend down to drink from the water fountain outside the bathroom door and hear sobbing echoing from the women's room.

You look at the empty bathroom doorway, wondering if you should ask if this person needs any help. The sobbing is shrill and wails up and down. Your station mate has arrived outside the bathroom door. He is speaking to the woman in rapid Spanish. You can only make out pieces of words and can only imagine what they are saying to each other. You decide it's best to go to lunch and let them handle it.

In the break room, you eat your pastrami sandwich on a pretzel bun, the same sandwich you have eaten every day at noon for months and will do so for years. You look out the window to the sunshine of the afternoon, then back out the break-room door to the gloom of the factory. People are playing music on their phones and heating up meals in the microwaves, talking in foreign languages that blend together with the background noise.

You think about the isolation of your work station, how you are contractually not supposed to talk to your coworkers or listen to music during your shift. You imagine being in a situation where you have to grieve, stuck wrenching valves in silence for eight hours while drills go off and forklifts beep by you carrying pallets of shipments.

Lunch is over and you are back at your station. Your station mate is working on building some eyewashes, attaching nozzles and craning the necks to the perfect angle in a vise grip. He makes no mention of the sobbing woman, but you have to ask.

"What was that?"

"What was what?"

"The sobbing earlier. Is that woman okay?"

"That was my wife," he tells you. "Her father just passed away."

"And she has to work?"

"Yes. We need the money." He says this and makes no more mention of the situation for the rest of the day.

* * *

Dreams are as meaningless as life itself. In this meaninglessness, you must find the answers. You dream of assembling valves as often as you dream of all the people who ever hated you. These days it is only on occasion that a dream stands out as profound. You dream now that your soul is separated from your body in two parallel dimensions.

Your body sits at a dining table in a decadent, antiquated mansion next to men and women your age whom you do not recognize. Your soul is running through a field of tall grass in a pack of equally desperate apparitions. Chased by some form of demon, your soul whispers childhood memories into loose branches of trees, lacing the bark in an attempt to wake the body. Your soul throws these branches up into the sky, and they silently disappear into the heavens.

In the other dimension, your spine receives tingling shocks, having been struck by the memory branches. Your body starts to become aware of not only the present situation but its forgotten past. This is when your back endures a deluge of sensation much like the popping of bulging zits. You look to your shoulder, which is now dotted with holes. The heads of purple earthworms peer out of the craters in your pores.

You pinch the worms in your fingers and pull them out of your back. The uneasiness that comes with this motion is enough to induce vomit. The worms are long, and it is hard to fully pry them out. As your body disgorges them, the memories whispered into the tree branches travel through the dimensions. You remove more slimy invertebrates from your right bicep and become aware of the fact that your body is being held captive in this mansion by a higher, darker being.

This same realization is dawning on the strange men and women around you. The more memories that are retrieved, the more the mansion crumbles into a desolate landscape. Whatever is holding you there is approaching. The experience reminds you that you once had a soul and that your soul is detached from your physical self. The air is thick with the dread of impending violence. You turn to run.

The woman next to you is screaming, sobbing in disbelief, puking out hundreds of discolored earthworms into her palms, eyes bulging.

* * *

You haven't seen your wife in five years, since the day you separated. You haven't talked to her in almost a year. So it is a surprise when you get a call from her lawyer at 6 a.m., telling you your court date is in five minutes. You received an email from a random address the evening before in all caps and 32-point bold font:

TESTING. TESTING.

You replied with an email reading, "Testing worked," and thought nothing of it before falling asleep.

Now your ex's lawyer is telling you he did everything he could to get ahold of you. Due to the COVID-19 pandemic, you must appear on a Zoom video chat meeting at 6:05 a.m. in front of a judge and 10 other couples who are also going through divorce procedures with their attorneys. You throw on a dirty tank top and try to comb your hair. Your face is unshaven. Your skin is yellow from drinking. Bags hang under your sunken eyes.

Most of the other people in the Zoom chat are just as disheveled as you. Your ex-wife, however, is done up in full makeup. Her hair shimmers in the light of her upscale apartment's kitchen. She is dressed like she is going to church. Her eyes are soft and vulnerable, like that of a fawn.

Your dog is barking in the background of your ex-wife's kitchen. His graying snout and cropped ears briefly jog by her stainless-steel industrial refrigerator, followed by his curling tail. You haven't seen your dog since the day you left your old place. Flipping through scrapbook photos of you holding him as a wide-eyed, big-pawed puppy helps get you through your toughest nights. You un-mute yourself in the chat and call his name. The judge reprimands you as if you are a naughty child.

In the other squares of broken-hearted faces, women and men are crying just the same. You are witnessing a tragic and often pathetic side of humanity that you always heard happened but never imagined happening to you. You feel nothing but a dull pain in your gut, burping out last night's pale lagers in the dim light of your kitchenette, which shades your face like a rail-riding hobo.

You have said "Yes, your honor" seven times but aren't even paying attention to what the judge is saying. You pour yourself a shot of vodka and hope that no one notices, though part of you hopes they actually do. When all is said and done, your ex-wife's lawyer assures you he will email you all the necessary information ASAP.

Five hours later, on break at work, you receive an email in bold font bearing only one sentence:

YOU ARE NOW DIVORCED.

* * *

"It's your first time working in a factory?" You have worked together long enough for your station mate to ask you about yourself.

"Yup, first time."

"Well, you're doing a good job."

"Thanks. Say, how long you been here?"

"You don't want to know."

"No?"

"Thirty years."

His cheeks are draped in wrinkles, hair balding into a horseshoe crown, brown eyes deep with stoicism. You nod your head. You have made no emotional connections since your hire. Not even a mutual sense of frustration. Just endurance.

Each day when you leave the factory, your face is smushed into a narrow-eyed sneer. People passing on the street gawk at the sight of you, like you might do them harm, like you might be crazy. But you are not angry.

You are not sad. You feel nothing. You are merely enduring the days like the rest of them. You pass the evening watching '80s movies and resting your aching bones.

Time is a primitive tool carving away at a granite slab. The more you lose from life, the more distinguished of a shape your identity adopts. You are lost in your own reflection, washing the thick gunk from your knuckles on break. Your face is hardened with time. You no longer resemble your childhood. You once knew yourself to be handsome, but your blue eyes are now iced over with the indifference of the city streets.

The wrench has turned enough in your palms to build heavy callouses on your fingers. You clench a fist and feel the added thickness of your skin. Your station mate is observing you analyze the cracks in your hands while he screws metal sheets together with a power drill.

"What did you do before this?" he asks.

"I've done a bunch of odd jobs. But most recently I was a bartender," you tell him, which is mostly a lie because to be a bartender was your intention before you were instead hired as a bouncer. The bar owner assured that you could work your way up. Years passed and the opportunity never came.

"You have to go to school for that? Must have to learn a lot of recipes."

"Nah."

"You don't like it?"

"I saw an ugly side of otherwise good people."

"Break up a lot of fights, eh?"

"Yeah, stupid shit. Had my share of beatings."

"So, you drink?"

"What, at work?"

The look on your station mate's face shows it: your tone revealed that you do drink at work, and he says nothing more. You remember the gold cross that dangles off his neck when he changes in the locker room at the end of each workday, the Police Union magnet that clings to his door, and you realize the question he asked was meant to be a judge of character and not an invitation for a nightcap.

"Well, I used to have a problem with it, but that was in my twenties. I got too far into it," you tell him, though he is hardly listening over the buzzing of his drill. "Now it's nothing more than a beer or two."

* * *

Solace is the balance of lies and lived experiences. Your pint has been refilled with gold lager at least six times this night. "ZAKOPANE: THE LITTLE TOWN IN THE MOUNTAINS" the faded sign outside reads, creaking in the wind.

"Zak-oh-pain!" Your facetious shout echoes through the empty room. No music has played since you got there. You slam your glass on the bar after a deep swig.

"Zah-ko-pah-nah," the old man behind the counter corrects you. His gray hair sticks out in random clumps from the side of his head. His cheeks sag with just as much exaggeration as his gut. "This street here, Division," he tells you in an accent, "used to be Little Poland. Polka bands would walk up and down the street, playing in the restaurants and taverns. People came from all over to see it. And Milwaukee Ave. was Polish Broadway. You would never know. It's all rich now. Poles moved out west on Belmont towards the suburbs. Just me and the old lady at Podhalanka by the triangle are left."

Nodding is all you can do to commiserate with him. Your eyes are heavy, and it is only 9 p.m. Your body leans forward into slumber and shoots back up to a superficial alertness before the old man looks to you.

"Actually, where you work on the North Branch is the heart of Stara Polonia, the original settlement in Chicago. Tanneries, meatpackers, coal companies, foundries, all there. They even built ships on the river. For North Side at least. South had the slaughterhouses in Back of the Yards. Used to be a gang of over 2,000 Poles down there, the Rebels. Real greaser motherfuckers."

"Lotta history," you say to him, nodding again.

"No one come in today. You only one," he tells you. You are sucking the last drops of beer from your glass like it is a canteen of water in the endless sands of a desert. "I close early. I close now. Go home." You plead with him to get a shot for the road, too drunk to feel pathetic. He shakes his head, denying you, turns on all the lights, and shoos you out the door. The mucus you spit onto the sidewalk serves as a lament to the grave of a working-class neighborhood, now ravished and squeezed dry of all culture by real-estate developers and Sunday brunch-goers who dared not tread on what this street once was.

* * *

Silhouettes of geese pass the sun shades of the factory window on the river side. You pause from turning your wrench on the valve and watch. They honk in a primal cacophony. Their gray bodies float up the 20-foot span of the shades, their wings flapping in an agitated hysteria. Squealing gulls swoop into the din, competing with the geese for turf and discarded food.

You imagine this moment in a movie. It is the closest thing to poetry you have seen in months. It should be enough to swell your heart, but there is only a curiosity, trying to picture this scene in black and white, a romantic film, during the Golden Age of cinema. You notice the factory owner eyeing you from the second-level balcony, holding a pen and clipboard. Your hands still grip the wrench tight. You begin to turn it again as if you had never stopped.

* * *

You start to grow suspicious of your coworkers, taking note of the tone of their conversations. You don't speak their language, and they rarely address you. But when a woman walks by, you make out the word "cula," and when you walk by, you make out the words "pendejo" and "*something something* mi verga"

You are excited to greet the two new Slavic assemblers. Maybe they will accept you. You ask if they are Russian. They say they are from Ukraine and Moldova.

"Where is Moldova?" you ask.

"Next to Ukraine," replies the Ukrainian.

"What do you call a person from Moldova?"

"What?" says the Moldovan.

You want to tell them you are Polish, but you hear the thickness of their accents and witness the continental distance behind their skewed eyes, and it dawns on you that you are not Polish. You are American. An American with a sense of "Polskość". *Polishness*. You realize you have no culture to call your own and start to question your identity. You decide you must come to terms with this fact:

Identity is the ripped skin lining your inner knuckles, overgrowing with callouses.

* * *

"Hey, Aulina!" you call your ex-girlfriend on the phone one day.

"Hey ... hey! What's up?" She brings her voice down into a whisper.

"It's been a while. I thought maybe we could get a drink and catch up sometime."

"Hey, yeah ... maybe ..."

"Ey! Who you talking to?" a man's voice calls from off in the distance of her apartment.

"Jesus Christ, Joe! I ain't talking to nobody!"

"What, you're just in the kitchen talking to yourself?"

"Aulina ..." you say again. The phone beeps, and you are left alone on your couch facing the silence.

* * *

You are dunking your valves in a sink filled with water, watching for air bubbles to rise up from the connection points to check for leaks. The bell for your lunch break rings. You pull out the valve and remove the tubes connected to the sink nozzle, rip off your latex gloves and toss them in the trash.

You begin walking toward the break room down the factory aisle past all the assemblers, each working a small job in a greater whole. You enter the stock area where stacks and stacks of material are wrapped in heavy-duty plastic on sheets of wood reaching up to the ceiling, only to be pulled down by forklift operators that scoot by you with deep expressions of boredom upon their faces.

Instead of walking to the bathroom to wash the gunk off your hands and go eat, you head to your locker and dial in your combination. You take out your flight jacket and put it on. Then you walk down the hall, past the break room, past the clock-in station, and out the front door into the daylight.

"Shit ..." you mutter to yourself. "Godamnit ... skurwysyn, prze-palanka ... fucking burnout ..." You have broken another promise. You rap your clenched fist to the side of your head in frustration, not knowing how you will explain this to your mother.

You walk south on North Branch through the empty industrial corridor, past honking geese, past trucks idling at loading docks. On Halsted, you look to your left, and the skyscrapers of downtown corporations shine in the late-morning light, stretching up into the clouds. You look to your right and a looming black chute of a nearby factory descends a couple hundred feet diagonally in front of pouting smokestacks over the curve of the Chicago River.

Jesus Christ, you're a fool …

You walk aimlessly, not even exactly sure why you left, only turning west once you get to Chicago Avenue. You are staring at all the pedestrians, jealous of their freedom, trying to tell yourself that you have your daytime freedom now too. That it will all be better. Maybe she will understand.

You pass boutique clothing stores and pizza shops, CTA Blue Line stops and tattoo parlors. You make your way all the way up to Ashland, past Alcala's Western Wear and the giant sign of a cowboy riding a horse with a lasso, lit up by large white bulbs.

Past Damen Avenue, you stop in at Kasia's Deli and order yourself a chicken Kiev and kopytka dumplings. The server is rude to you, but you do not care. You tell yourself you do not care about anything right now. You receive a phone call but let it go to voicemail. Your coworkers should have already gone back from lunch to find you missing over 15 minutes ago.

The chicken Kiev was heated up in the microwave, and the spinach inside is cold, but you eat it ravenously. The gunk from the valves left on your fingers smears into the food, but it does not bother you. You left your pastrami sandwich in your locker to rot.

When you finish eating, you take the Damen bus back to the South Side and make your way home to sit in your apartment and relax. You don't do much of anything, just enjoy the afternoon. You go to sleep at night trying to be excited for a new chapter in your life. You feel guilty for the way you left, but you needed to focus on bettering yourself. That place sucked the life out of you. It wasn't viable.

* * *

In the morning you get a call from work. You imagine it will be the manager calling to fire you, but you answer anyway. It is an automated call letting you know you have used one of your sick days and you only have a certain number left throughout the year. You are confused to find out that you still work at the factory. The fact that they weren't mad astounds you. Sobered by the daylight, you realize you need to keep this job. You don't have a backup plan or any money to start fresh. You put on your clothes and hop on the bus to Division and walk the same walk you have walked for the longest time, down past the iron bridges and the bending river, where the geese congregate to shit, eat, honk, and fight. You clock back into work like nothing happened. No one mentions anything. They hardly cared you were gone.

* * *

It is Christmas Eve, and you are at your mother's house in Archer Heights drinking brown glasses of Susz. She reaches in the cupboard and pulls out an opłatek wafer. You have just returned from Wigilia mass together at St. Stanilslaus Kostka. At her age it is a pilgrimage to the North Side. So you helped her in a cab and accompanied her to the first Polish church in Chicago. Your mother breaks a piece off the opłatek and places it on her tongue, praying for your happiness and health in the coming new year.

"My son," she adds, "I hope this year is the start of new love for you. Not just love in new woman...But love in yourself. Here's what I say is wrong with you! You try get serious with woman, try and get married, settle down, yeah? But you never learned self-respect. You are little boy in a grown man's body. You have these blessings that I never have. And you toss them aside like it wasn't from *sacrifice*? It's love I wish for you, and tough love I give to you in return!"

"Well, Mom," you say, breaking off a piece of the wafer and letting it dissolve in the back of your mouth, "in this new year ... I guess I just hope I can make you happy."

Planes are taking off by Midway Airport, interrupting your conversation every number of minutes. They are the planes you used to watch while lying on the sidewalks of your neighborhood, guessing against your friends the far-off places that they might go as they blinked and blended into the dots of stars.

Ignacy Jan Paderewski piano concertos play on your mother's radio. She has made white borscht with sausage, carp fillet, kapusta, and a plate of gołąbki. The stuffed cabbage rolls have been your favorite since you were a teenager. You scarf them down, responding to your mother through mouthfuls of food.

You look up from your plate to see her hands shake as she cuts the carp with her silver fork and knife. You analyze the off-white wrinkles in her face and the dangling skin of her sagging throat, and it hits you that you don't know how many Christmas Eves you will have left together. You wish you would have gotten to know her in adulthood on a more personal level, but you have always been working or drinking or chasing girls. The richness of the food cannot mask the bitter flavor of regret lumped back behind your tonsils.

"For your father," she says, pouring you a glass of homemade spirytus rektyfikowany and a sip of krupnik for herself. You clink your drinks together, and before the 192-proof grain alcohol tingles your lips, wets your tongue, and burns the back of your throat, you recall the last time you saw your father.

Your mother takes your empty glasses to the sink and washes them, though there is still food left to eat on her plate.

* * *

Heaven is the inside of an all-night diner during a December snowstorm. God is the old waitress calling you hon' and offering you a creamy soup of cheese and potatoes in a throaty Chicago accent. You are reminded of a painting called *Nighthawks* you once saw at the Art Institute downtown, supposedly one of the first existentialist pieces in the art world. You didn't think much of it then, but you believe you understand it now.

The light of the diner glows into the empty streets. There is no life behind the stained glass of the gothic cathedral across the intersection. The snow is thick. Its downpour is relentless. You nurse your soup and watch the white dots blanket the black of the night like static on a television.

"More coffee, hon'?" the waitress asks.

There is a gentle smile in her face, though her lips fail to curve. She fills your cup. The steam rises from the mug, and you douse it with a packet of creamer. Christmas oldies are still playing on the radio. You remember past South Side Christmases from this North Side red vinyl booth and watch the cream pies rotate lazily in the display case by the register.

* * *

The holidays are over. You are back to work. "Another fuckin' day," says a forklift operator, clocking in, still wearing his bike helmet strapped around his chin. His feet are tracking in brown muck mixed with slushy snow.

"How old are you?"

"Twenty-five," he says.

Youth is a sacrifice to the hands of an apathetic God. Some do not see a purpose in the rolling of the dice. You witness the soul detach from the forklift operator's face, his physical body still present, now hollow. You stuff your olive-green bomber jacket into your locker, slam the door, and click the padlock shut. Walking out onto the factory floor for *another fuckin' day,* you realize: This factory does not manufacture faucets out of brass valves. It manufactures shells out of young men.

ATLANTYCKI

In your right hand is a lightning whelk shell wreathed in grains of sand. The pale color is not too far off from the neutral tones of your own flesh. The spiral tightens to a conical point at its base and unfurls wider like a rolled-up newspaper toward the top. Its outside is circularly lined with jagged, white spikes. The ocean wind blows through the whelk's empty cavern, producing a soft whistle that sounds much like the waves in front of you when placed up to your ear.

The sun is an orange rose blooming over the emerald meadows of the Atlantic, white with froth and foam. Its fiery petals thrust their rays, sharp as sabers, through the purple shades of the cotton clouds. The pink orb rises into a dandelion crown above the perpetually swirling brine, while echoed cries of brown pelicans sound out as they swoop across the salty spray of waves. Toward the horizon, fishing ships linger, trolling as a fleet on the span of open water.

"Spider!" a woman calls out to you. Her familiar voice is muffled by the wind and the crashing of the breakers. You turn to see your dog sprinting toward you, a boxer with cropped ears and a wiry tail, barking playfully, kicking wet sand, black pouches of stranded shark eggs, and broken quahog shells in the wake of his spotted paws. Behind him, your wife is waving at you down the shoreline. Her bare feet disappear in the thin veil of water rolling up the slope of the beach. Your dog bounds and leaps over a pile of seaweed and faded driftwood, swept up the sand from the night's high tide, now drying in the sun.

The scene feels like a memory filmed on Super 8, though you are sure it is happening right before your eyes. It is almost as if you had never met your wife before this moment, never had the joy of greeting your jovial dog, never stood on this empty beach whose sounds drone on like a pink noise track made to help the petite bourgeoisie sleep under puffed, white comforters and fluffy, white pillows, in stainless glass-paneled apartments, built on the rubble of timeless Americana. Despite these doubts and the abstruse happenstance of this situation, you see your wife's smiling face, her vulnerable chestnut eyes, umber locks of hair, pale skin soaked red with sun, and for the first time in so long you are truly happy.

* * *

You are knee deep in the shallows of Barnegat Bay, watching groups of minnows dart around the plunging feet of the other kids romping beside you. You sweep your hand into the murky water and clench a fist to catch a fish and miss. Your mother is calling your name from the shoreline, lying back on a striped blanket, in a straw sunhat and black shaded glasses, on the sand of the miniature beach alongside other lounging parents watching their children swim. Behind her are a small parking lot and a wooden playground shaped like a line of train cars from locomotive to caboose in which kids scamper in and out, like slinking river rats, playing tag.

You are looking out to the open water of the bay. The concept of its depth is enough to speed up the beating of your heart. It is like being on your back in a field of grass, feeling the vertigo of staring up into the endless sky. It is akin to imagining life after death, pondering eternity. Luckily, the bay area is enclosed in a square of wooden planks lined with wire. At each post in the water is a gull, bathing in the sun, squawking, nipping its feathers, fluttering its wings in aggravated discourse, like bickering New Yorkers, like old married couples. You wonder if the sharks can get in through the boards. You were misfortunate enough to have seen *Jaws* on TV before your family's trip to the shore, and now your perception of the way the ocean works has been tainted for the remainder of your childhood.

Your mother calls your name again, but you'd rather pay attention to the little blue crab you see scuttling out toward the end of the enclosure past the tufts of seaweed, mussels, and half-buried hermit shells. A child splashes you and shrieks in laughter, producing a gust of sand that bursts under the water. You wipe your face, tasting traces of the bitter Atlantic on your lips, still stained red and blue from Bomb Pops purchased from an ice cream truck blaring nursery rhymes, after a guilt trip and an exchange of quarters from adult to child's hands. You continue to stumble forward in pursuit of the crab. When you find it again, its antennae eyes watch you blankly. It scuffs backwards, clicking its orange-green claws.

The sun is beating down on your back. You can feel the burn setting in, the red skin beginning to peel white. Your hair is matted to your ears and brow. Your mother shouts now. All you know is you want the crab. The water is higher in this part of the bay beach, almost up to your waist. Just as you think you have your opportunity to pounce on the tiny crustacean, your foot catches on a broken shell. Your body trips forward as you whine in pain, your open mouth connecting with the brine of the water in time for you to submerge in a scattered explosion of oxygen bubbles, throat choking on salt, eyes burning wide open in a thick, disorienting green. Maroon fluid curls from the bottom of your heel like smoke from the end of a cigarette.

This blood will attract the sharks.

* * *

The lighthouse is operated by the ghosts of dead seamen. The rotating tower beams are the illuminations of their incorporeal eyes. The groaning steel is the moan of shanties to the fishing ships on the bleak horizon. It is the lullaby of the apparitions. It is sung almost hopefully, like a prayer for good luck.

The same stars watch these same lights upon the inlet's coast every night as the waves roughen and crash upon the rocks of the jetty at the house's base. The stars are junkyard dogs. North glows the brightest. He leads the pack. He knows what the others don't, why they must shine, why the churning lights of the dead upon the Atlantic deserve protecting, deserve respect.

You can see the lighthouse from your bedroom. At night it is the brightest being in the town. A maritime skyscraper. A temple for the perpetual currents. You can't sleep. This is not your room. That is not your closet. The streets of Chicago are never this dark. In Archer Heights the ghosts are familiar. You have made friends with the monsters under your bed.

In the town of Barnegat Light, the ghosts are older, sadder, the kind that carry heavy chains. Nineteen of them were sailor men murdered on the beach in their sleep by Bacon and the loyalists during the American Revolution. They cry to you the loudest while you try to close your eyes. Their mourning is profound. They miss their wives and children.

The heel of your foot is bandaged from the afternoon. You remember the depths of the waters in front of you and fight the oncoming vertigo. The wind is fluttering the grass reeds of the dunes outside your window. On it you hear voices. In the reeds you make out faces. The leagues of the ocean are engulfing you, and before you know it, the lament of the deceased has silenced, and you are trenched in slumber.

The lighthouse on the point groans, churns, and weeps luminosity above the quaint pastel cottages and pebble driveways littered with nettles of Japanese black pines. It is manned by the souls of those who vowed marriage to the sea.

* * *

Sixteenth Street in Barnegat is nothing like the 16th Street of Chicago. In fact, 16th Street in Barnegat is nothing like it was in the 1990s. The modest off-color cottages, stained green by the bite of the sea breeze, were mostly annihilated by a hurricane. Real-estate developers swooped in after the tragedy to build luxury condos and three-story beach mansions draped in "TRUMP 2020" flags and "Blue Lives Matter" banners.

Pebble backyards with swaying clothes lines, dilapidated tool sheds, and outdoor showers built from wooden planks are now peanut shaped in-ground pools with home tiki bars and "man-cave" guest houses attached to two-car garages. The widow's walks wrapping the homes of the colonial Mid-Atlantic, where brooding wives scanned the horizon over the rolling dunes for signs of their husbands' return from across the sea, are now rooftop balconies for the well fed to feed on fish, white wine, martinis, at glass tables and patio chairs, lusting over friends' spouses who dance to Tom Petty over the loud speakers, wishing their own wife could be that tempting, that free, while the rest of the neighborhood dims their lights and tries to sleep.

You turn from 16th Street on to Ocean County Road. A lifted truck speeds by, shouting something in your direction. You piece together that you have just been called a "fag." You turn and watch the novelty testicles swing from the back of his trailer hitch as he heads down the main strip of town towards Mustache Bill's Diner. You are trying to imagine how any woman could live with such a man or how such a man could even live with himself.

On Bayview Avenue, the docked motor boats of the marina sway in the lolling of the waves, tethered to wooden stakes plagued with mussel shells and barnacles. This is where you see the last remnants of the old way of life upon the shore.

From a wooden shack, four men are watching you, lazily chewing tobacco, grimacing, though this is just the way the years have shaped their jaws. Their faces are tanned leather from a life in the sun, like a catcher's mitt, like the skin of a football. They wear fisherman's caps and plain faded shirts. They are unimpressed by you. They are unamused with the world. Chartering boats is their trade. Their shack is cluttered with equipment.

You now know what it is like to witness one of a kind, the last of a dying breed. These men were born upon the sea and will die upon the sea. The words of their life stories end with the lines of the town. The rest of the universe is of little interest. It sits beyond their minds as a place holder, taking up space.

You are now walking alongside a thicket of 10-foot-tall golden reeds lining the bay. At points you can see through to the water. At 23rd Street you notice a discrete trail beaten between the reeds, and on impulse you crawl in.

The ground is moist with sand and mud beneath your feet. The reeds nip your cheeks, prod at your brow, and tickle the top of your scalp. A stream of water runs through the thicket. You hop from rock to rock, trying not to slip, eventually exiting the path onto a bar of sand.

You are watching the minnows dart in the shallows, remembering being a child. Your wife and dog are far away. It has all come down to this, a pensive isolation. The small blue crabs scuttle sideways through the weeds with black-beaded eyes staring off at nothing at all. Two large ospreys perch like royalty on a dinghy anchored twenty feet out. They are a triumphant white and gray with dignified hooked beaks, knuckled talons, and razor eyes.

The high tide has washed carcasses of deceased creatures onto the shore. As you nurse the coastline headed south for no particular reason, you discover their bodies one by one. Your self-reflection in their demise is the closest thing they receive to a funeral rite.

By your feet is the shell of an enormous horseshoe crab. Its face is a vacant grey-brown dome backed with lines of spikes and a stiff pointed tail that reminds you of the nose of a swordfish. In a few attempts, you kick the shell over to reveal the meaty rows of spider legs, the only aesthetic piece of this being that actually resembles a crab. The image of your wife and dog greeting you during the morning calm enters your head, and on an impulse, you raise and drop your foot down into the horseshoe's shell, stomping its body inside itself. You leave it there crumpled and gnarled.

Next is the carcass of a sea turtle, half eaten by scavengers during the morning hours. It is missing its face and most of its stomach. Along the sand you find smaller turtles, equally ravaged. Hermit crabs aimlessly scoot across their bellies. You become so focused on counting the casually rotting corpses around you that you hardly notice where it is you have walked to.

You are on the outside of an enclosure on the water. Wooden planks strung together with wire jut out on to the bay,. Small pillars line the corners. On each post sits a gull. Their shrieks resemble the squeal of a rusted metal swing. Your feet sink into mud as you turn around the bend. You raise one leg over the fenced enclosure, swing your hip and raise the other. The beach is as it always was, but children no longer play along the shore. The wooden locomotive play set is old and falling apart. The area is entirely empty. You disgust yourself when tears come to your eyes. You try to choke them down and be a man, like there is anyone watching. You are unsure why you are angry. You remember how much you miss your mother.

* * *

"No, we can't swim right now. The sharks feed at dusk."

You and your wife are sitting next to each other in two wooden lifeguard chairs once painted ruby red, now chipped with time. You have had a six pack of Narragansett between the two of you, and climbing the 10-foot posts was a challenge. Now your hand is on her lap. Each of you holds a sweating bottle of Yuengling, a Midwest booze-hound's plunder of the East Coast. The repetition of the waves relaxes you. The moon romances. Its light glistens upon the water. You were discussing stripping down and bathing in the darkness. But you saw *Jaws* when you were young.

"C'mon, just for a few minutes. It'll be fine." Your wife kisses you. You reluctantly take off your shirt just as voices sound out from the path through the dunes, followed by lights of smart phones and girlish teenage laughter. "Fuck ..."

Six high school girls now stand around the lifeguard chairs, playing Top 40 pop hits on their phone speakers and dancing poorly. One of them climbs the chair and sits next to you, though she doesn't acknowledge your presence. Another two are staring at your wife's chair expectantly.

"Here, let them sit down," you say. "You guys wanna sit down?"

"Thanks, sir."

"Ah, shit, I'm that old."

"Huh?"

"I'm getting called sir now."

"What are you kids doing out this late?" your wife asks.

"It's my 18th birthday," says a girl taking your wife's place on the wood post, "Our parents went to bed, so we're out here celebrating." Another girl has opened her backpack and is passing out Mike's Hard Lemonade to her friends. You and your wife are nudging each other, amused by the teens' authentic Jersey accents and exaggerated mannerisms.

"I miss being young," she says to you.

"How old are you?" interrupts one of the girls.

"Eh ... I'd rather not say. But, hey ... I'm still cool! I can still party!" The girls laugh at this.

"Yeah, you're still cool!" You rub your fist in your wife's hair and laugh when she screams. "C'mon." You take your wife's hand and walk her back up the dunes in silence. "You know this place ... this place is like a Neverland to me. To come here from Chicago, in my father's car. Maybe 14 hours. As a kid, it was so different. It was a fairy tale. I feel like the Peter Pan who left and got old. Came back jaded."

"Better than if you stayed a kid."

"Is it?"

"When Wendy grew up and became a mother and she saw Peter still a little boy, she pitied him. Their love was distant, maternal, not romantic. It's foolish to want to be young forever."

"So you're my Wendy, huh?"

"Childhood is only good if it ends, Spider."

"I miss my dad."

"Oh, don't get started ..."

Your wife puts her arm around your shoulder. You look back to the beachfront, the moonlight rippling on the waves, then to the tall grass sprouting from the sand around you. In one of the trees, an intricate spider web spans a couple feet, glistening like a diamond. It evokes a greater sense of melancholy into your intoxicated state.

Across the island, the lights of the coastal homes slowly shut off, making way for the blanket of stars, an ocean in their own right. At the point of the inlet between the bay and the open water, Old Barney, the red and white painted lighthouse, now a phallic silhouette, churns its rays in a spiral. You try to feel the same sense of awe you had as a child here on this same beach, this same dune, watching this light that turns and turns and lives as long as there is a dark night to expose, and you know your Neverland is tainted, and you can never go back to what it was.

* * *

It has rained through the evening. All that's left is Aulina's cigarette trail blowing out in the mist that swells from the base of Chicago's downtown. She looks out toward the skyscrapers, half shrouded in white. The lights of offices puncture through at various points. You can't help but think of the ships resting on the black of the open sea. You can't help but think of yourself as a child.

The church tower you are in stands like a lighthouse across Pilsen. It is a point of reference. An icon. You dress yourself in your jeans and shoes and approach Aulina from behind, resting your hands on her naked hips. You slowly draw them up her soft skin to fit under the crease of her exposed breasts against her ribs.

She turns her head back over her shoulder and kisses you. Sensually. Like your wife hadn't done in so long. This feels right. It is a place where wrong and right meet that disorients you into a raw lingering guilt. You are sick with nerves. You are consumed with grief and affection and longing while you climb down the scaffolding with her and kiss her once more before splitting ways through the neighborhood.

* * *

Under the flickering street lights of Andy's General Store, the stray cats of Barnegat congregate in a wailing din of *meows* to sleep, fight, fuck, and cuddle in a pile of fur and curling tails, long hair, short hair, orange, gray, black, white, brown, with the jaded eyes of Egyptian gods, green and yellow, black pupils growing wide as saucers, pale claws protruding from teddy bear paws, sharp as a pocket knife, dirty with sand and debris, they make their ways to the painted wooden hutches built for them to brave the elements, and the whole island is sleeping, save a few insomniacs and old couples fearing death (their kids don't call), so the spiraling beacon of Old Barney and this sputtering streetlight illuminate the night of the greatest party no person has ever attended, a wordless station of debauchery where kittens become cats and cats produce kittens, some missing eyes from street scraps, others clipped on the ear, some with matted fur, or fleas, or ear mites, or AIDS, but all proud regardless to be killers, under the stars, and above the law of humans, scrounging through the trash cans to sit on the laps of the gods.

* * *

This is not Jerusalem. This is New Jersey.

The hulking anchor bearing down on your bare back is the closest thing you will carry to a crucifix. Your spine is crouched in pain under the weight. The metal point that drags behind you draws a traceable line in the hot sand, which burns the skin under your feet. Your only clothes are your swim trunks with a mesh hammock built in to serve as underwear. Pink starfish and red crabs dangle from your limbs and the curled hair of your chest with vacuum suction cups and pinched claws.

A whip snaps with a crisp crack, and a braided rope of seaweed strung with sharp shells and shark's teeth slashes your back and draws drips of claret from your skin like paint rolling down a wall. You now notice the crowd around you, watching you trudge the path through the dunes. Leather-faced fishermen draw their whips and snap them under the scalding sun. Widows who walked the balconies praying their men weren't consumed by the sea now weep at the sight of your pathetic march. One holds a beach towel stained with the image of your face. The anchor is getting harder and harder to hold. You fall not once but twice.

On your head is a crown of barnacles and clumps of mussel shells. Your cheeks and chin are adorned with a thick beard, perhaps entirely composed of sand. Gulls dive and peck at your eyes, your hair, bite loose chunks of skin. You cried in pain at first, but now all you do is wince.

The crowd is larger on the beach. It is a sweaty summer afternoon. A lifeguard comes to help carry the burden of your anchor. His cheeks are smeared with lines of white lotion like the grease strip of a linebacker. Upon seeing this, the old fishermen and charterers of boats step in to beat him down. He is a tourist with a beach pass and a part-time job. Their blood is diluted green and bitter with salinity. When they are finished, the lifeguard's body is crumpled like a piece of scratch paper to be thrown into a waste bin. You are whipped again and urged to continue.

Dolphins are arcing out of the water in joyous flips in the distance. They have come to watch a good man die. A child on the sidelines tosses a yellow, red, and white beach ball at your head. He cries as it bounces off the edge of a barnacle on your crown and deflates into a pool of wrinkled plastic on the ground.

Your feet are in the water now. It is cold, and goosebumps line your skin. The crowd no longer weeps and jeers. Their hands are in the air, waving gently like the Queen of England. They resemble monstrous dandelions, as does the sun. You should be able to stand at this depth, but the anchor drags you down below the oncoming waves. Shark fins are cutting towards you across the water, fast like bullets, black in austerity. For once this doesn't scare you. Maybe you won't have to drown.

All that is left above the surface is the crown on your forehead.

You struggle above the water to suck in a breath. You scream as rows of jagged teeth sink into your leg, your torn limb burning in the salt. The last of the fight is out of you. The anchor is dragging you down to the sharks. The last thing you see above the water before slipping into the undertow is a small aircraft spiraling smoke into the sky. It has written out a series of words.

You cry out from another shark bite. Water plunges into your lungs. By the time the aircraft has finished its message your soul has disconnected from the physical world. The pilot removes his goggles and turns his head behind him to admire the skill of his work, a loop of clouds, the job of three men, tactfully done, spelling the encouraging message:

BETTER LUCK NEXT TIME!

* * *

You are on your knees in the swash of the waves, waiting for the fore-wash to recede to dig your adolescent hands into the wet sand and pull out barrel-shelled bodies of mole crabs, "sand fleas," their tickling rows of legs thrashing frantically to escape, though you've gripped them tightly in your palm. You have collected about ten fleas now, their tan shells blending in with the sand of the orange bucket you have placed them in. They dig tail first, back into the bottom of the pail to hide. You scoop the bucket into the swash, and the ocean water floats the bugs (that didn't burrow) to the top, where they helplessly gyrate. You watch their brutal torture with the wondrous eyes of a child.

* * *

A stereo on the beach blanket next to you and your parents blares distorted guitar rhythms of 1980s pop rock groups while a middle-aged couple drunkenly dances and stumbles, grasping one another's hips, swaying in half time to amplified choruses and in-the-pocket bass and drum grooves. They have been playing this music for over an hour. It is louder than any other sound on the beach.

You look to your mother, who rolls her eyes. Your father shakes his head. You are leaning back on your right elbow, playing with a plastic shovel, digging into the sand with your left hand, to a soundtrack you didn't ask for, realizing the people occupying the space near you are intoxicated. Across the water, a motorboat drags the rainbow chute of a parasail and the strapped-in human across the sky, dipping them down to the surface before a pocket of wind bursts them back into the air.

The man kisses his woman. The top of his hair is thin and wiry, the remaining strands combed as best as he can across the sunburned skin of his scalp dotted with liver spots. The flesh of the woman's cheeks is sagging, though the bones under her eyes protrude in a dignified cut. You can tell she used to be very beautiful. Her green eyes are faded like the ocean spray. The endurance of a lifetime has dulled their color. Her blond hair is teased with combed-in product. Her small bronzed breasts, once plump, now droop and wrinkle in her striped blue and white bikini.

"Aw, shut the fuck up, fer Christ's sake..." your father mutters, turning the page of his non-fiction bestseller on the life and times of Winston Churchill during the height of World War II.

"No different than taking Orange Line," your mother offers, puffing a cigarette.

"Psia krew!"

"Co?"

"Co? Chujow sto!"

"Dupa..."

"You speak Polish po Chicagosku," your father laughs, lightening up for a moment.

"So do you!" Your mother slaps him on the arm.

"No ..."

The couple is laughing heartily, and you imagine they are laughing at you. The man reaches down and feels the curves of his woman's ass, assuming you won't notice and not caring at all if you do. His collared shirt is too big for him. If it wasn't unbuttoned, it would hide his beer gut, dropping off his torso like a bead of sweat on the edge of a brow.

Duran Duran is playing. The couple knows all the words and sings along, no matter how offbeat or off key.

"I'm going to say something," your father says, putting down his book after marking his page with a pizza delivery flyer that was placed on the front door to the rental house that morning. The couple falls to the ground and rolls around, kissing. "A boy shouldn't have to see this," your dad says. You can't help but watch. You look closer and see a tear rolling down the man's cheek.

Your father stands up, but the couple has already turned off the stereo. They are packing up their gear, crying, with inebriated smiles.

"You—" your father begins to say, but the couple has already interrupted. The man has put his hands together like he is saying a prayer.

"Thank you so much for dealing with us," he says.

"Thanks?" your mother asks.

"You don't know what we've been through ..." the man continues.

"You've got a lot of nerve ..." Your father maintains his outrage.

"We've been through hell and back, but it's over. It's over now. We can finally breathe," says the woman, kissing the man's cheek. They carry their foldable chairs, towels, and blanket past your family, heading toward the dunes.

"If only you knew what we've been through for this," the man says, wiping tears from his eyes. "Thank you." Your father still wants to be mad, but he is too flustered to comprehend the situation. Before he can think of something to say, the couple is already in the distance. The man yells, "Woo! 'in a high pitch. The woman slaps his ass and laughs gayly. Your father sits back down in his chair, sighs, and grumbles, crosses his arms, and looks to you, then your mother, before picking his book back up, removing the paper-flyer bookmark, and continuing to read about the times that tried men's souls. You no longer play with your shovel in the sand. All you can do is stare out across the shoreline, past your shrugging mother and ill-tempered father, wondering about the kinds of things that lie ahead in adulthood that could draw a man to smile while shedding tears.

* * *

Your mother has taken you home from the bay. Using a cotton swab, she applies rubbing alcohol to the bottom of your foot as you wince in pain. She laughs a little as you do this, not at your suffering, but at your cuteness. She puts a bandage on your foot and wraps some medical tape around it then spanks you on the butt, inviting you to stand up.

It begins raining. The coastal type of rain that smells of salt. You and your parents sit on the screened-in porch of the rental home on a wicker bench rocking chair. The three of you sway back and forth in each other's arms watching the downpour pelt off the sandy pebbles. Across the dunes you can hear the ocean's roar.

You rest your head onto your mother's bosom. Your legs stretch across your father's lap. Your mother strokes your eyebrows rhythmically with her thumb, and your father grips your shins tight. Their conversation becomes white noise, one in the same with the rain.

"I love him," you hear your mother say.

"If there was any softness to become of me, this boy is that." Your father runs his fingers across your scalp. Your mother leans in and kisses your forehead. They carry you to the bedroom, and you keep your eyes shut, focusing on the sensation. The feeling. To always remember this moment.

* * *

You are sitting by yourself in a movie theater, bathing in the consuming light of the blurred picture on the screen. It reminds you of the light said to draw one to heaven by those who have experienced closeness to death. The people's heads around you are the faceless black of store-display mannequins. You feel almost sedated, abnormally calm.

You hear the sound of the entrance doors slapping shut. Your head turns instinctively to see a pale woman with golden blond hair. More so than the angel of death, which only briefly crosses your mind, she looks like Britney Spears, the closest reference to exalted beauty pop culture has fed down your throat at such a young age.

Fight or flight mode kicks in with a burst of fluttering butterflies producing electric waves through your chest and stomach. You look away, hoping she never noticed you watching her. You sink into your seat, gripping your stomach over the residual anxiety of the exchange of eyes.

The woman is sitting on your lap now. She strokes your arm and runs her fingers through your hair. You glance to the faceless plastic beings around you as if they would be watching or calling you out for your actions. The celestial light of the screen adorns this woman's head like a halo. It is too pure to be true. You remember the angel of death again. The pale horse. You think this might be the devil. But you know it is something different entirely. Something more complex than good and evil. Not a sin but an abstraction of desire, a morally gray area serving wants and needs over piety. The woman glides in to kiss your lips. You have now felt the fear and adrenaline of a victim of a homicide.

* * *

Your eyes open again, and you are unsure if you ever received this kiss. You are in the bedroom of the rental house in Barnegat. The night is over. The lost sailors manning the beacon on the jetty in nocturnal lamentations have faded back into the morning calm. Their cater-wauling is an echo in the ocean's recess of dreams. A pink clenched fist stretches its fingers into orange rays across the battalions of oncoming waves on the horizon, led by lunar pulls of tides indifferent to your dreams. Their religion is the clockwork of the earth. Overnight your religion has been irreparably shattered through biology.

You are more aware of your phallus than you ever have been before. The butterflies that were in your chest and belly now tingle its deflated skin under your boxers, though there is something new, something wet, slightly alarming, sticking your shorts and skin together, something you have never felt before but know will start to change everything inside and out of your life.

You recall the last semester of school when your teachers divided the class into girls and boys and sent both groups into separate rooms to learn about the changes in their bodies. They showed you a series of skits and medical photographs between clips of doctors talking about a word that you cannot at the moment recall. Mostly you remember the awkward laughter of the boys around you, the ones who had to make jokes to break the tension, to cool the confused rage of hormones spiring in their vessels. You joined along at all the right moments to maintain a sense of normalcy within the crowd, though you didn't understand a minute of it.

When the girls joined the boys again at the end of the day, a new discomfort had grown between the members of the class. Boisterous class clowns were now awkward and shy around girls whose hair they had pulled, had chased around at recess just days before. You asked each other what had been shown in those rooms, and neither party truly comprehended enough to share.

You slide the boxers down your knees. The sticky liquid glued to the cloth pulls on your skin as you take the shorts off. At first you hope you just wet the bed, but a small streak of white is stained onto your privates.

A heavy hand knocks on the door. You father calls your name to come eat breakfast. He asks if he can enter. You tell him no. He comes in anyway, the turn of the handle a ticking bomb before he finds you lying naked with this strange white stain on your body.

You rip the covers over your hips before he can see. "What's wrong?" your father asks. He sits down at your bedside and rubs the top of your hair. You are paralyzed with anxiety and wish he would go away.

"You look like you've seen a ghost, buddy!" Your father laughs. He sees in your face that it is something deeper. His smile draws down, and he asks more seriously, "Is everything all right, Boo Boo?" He calls you by your childhood nickname, for always having scrapes and bruises on your knees playing in the streets. You nod, assuring him that everything is fine, though you are more scared than you ever have been about the changes happening in your life, and you feel as though it is a dark depraved secret that must be kept inside until it bursts. It is yours alone to bear. You can never tell anyone. They wouldn't understand.

* * *

"Are you trying to make me look like an idiot?"

You yell at your wife with your hands to your head. You didn't swim today. Local sewage spilling into the coastline produced an algal bloom across the shore. A boom of reproducing algae, and toxic shellfish that have feasted upon them, has changed the tide from a foamy pine green to a murky brownish red through photosynthesis.

"What? I can't talk to other people?"

"It wasn't other people! It was another guy!"

"OK, Mr. Insecure! You got me all hyped up to swim, then had me sitting on the blanket while you had a panic attack."

"Those red tides can give you PSP!"

"What the fuck is PSP?"

"Paralytic Shellfish Poisoning!"

"Oh, for fuck's sake!"

"Even so, you were hitting on him right in front of me!"

"Would you rather I did it behind your back?"

"I'd rather you not do it at all! Fuck!" Your temper strands you way out of bounds, and before you realize what you have done, you have punched a hole in the drywall of the rental house. Your sleeping dog jolts up from his bed cushion, whimpers, and scampers down the hall. The silence that follows is sobering and shameful. You breathe heavily. Your wife groans in despair. You trail her like a duckling as she storms away.

"Honey, I'm sorry! I didn't mean to do that."

"Well, we're not getting our fucking deposit back. You're gonna pay for that, Spider—"

"OK! OK! I'll fix it up! I'll do anything! Don't leave!"

"I'm getting out of here for the day."

"Baby, c'mon. I'd never hurt you! I fucking love you!"

"..."

"Where are you going?"

"Out!"

"Baby, wait!"

Your wife has grabbed her purse and sunglasses, slipped her red-painted toes into tan sandals and slammed the front door behind her. You stare at the door as if its closure is impenetrable, as if this door is the reason your wife has gone out into the town alone, the reason she hates you right now, and this door stands like a guard holding you back, the bouncer of a club who lets the girlfriends in but keeps the drunk losers out in the streets, knowing their bodies are past their prime, and even in their prime would never be athletic enough to take on the man blocking the narrow path to fun. Fuck this door.

Through the kitchen window, you see your wife hastily crossing the pebble driveway, doing her best to be cautious about stubbing her feet. You spit at the glass pane, open the fridge and pull out a Yuengling lager. You open the bottle with your front teeth, an attempt to retain your manhood.

When you turn around you are faced with the reality of the hole you punched in the wall. Your heart drops. You have castrated yourself. You feel ashamed drinking a beer, like you have become a brute in a moment's time. A drunk. You put the beer down on the kitchen table, then consider that it's already been opened, so you sip it slowly on the rooftop balcony, watching the maroon red tide lurk under the blue skies of the Atlantic.

You will make your wife a nice dinner tonight. Stuffed shells with ricotta cheese. Get her a bottle of wine. Say sweet things. Maybe even buy a rawhide chew for the dog. Yes. That will do. And by the time she comes home, distance will have softened the blow. It will all be a funny story to tell later at parties. You just wish she wouldn't have talked to that young man on the beach towel next to you.

* * *

There is a hole in the wall of Aulina's apartment. A hole that you can't stop staring at every time you pass. After you fuck. After you eat. While you are watching TV. When you have people over for drinks. Aulina laughs and chats with her friends. She dances while they drink and sing and fall into the pots of ferns. Angry music blasts from speakers, and you imagine the sounds pulsating from the rage that caused that cave in the drywall. Aulina smiles and kisses your cheek. She has brought you a Fernet and Coke in a pint glass. The ice rattles around as she draws you from the living room into the kitchen to socialize.

* * *

You and your father had bought two box-caged crab traps from Andy's General Store, along with some cuts of flounder to place in the center. You stood together on the docks of the marina heaving your cages into the water beside the row of pastel sail boats and tethered speed cruisers, feeling the subtle bump and tug on the line clenched in your fists when the trap hit the floor of the bay.

Every so often you felt a tingle on the line and hoisted the rope to pull the trap into view. The first few times it was nothing. Then it was one, two, three, then crab after crab, you and your dad were hunting with magic flounder that could never be eaten, only desired, a mermaid's call, a siren song of crustaceans, your tall bucket soon grew heavy with the clutter of claws and shelled bodies, champing at the bit, tearing at each other, pushing others down to make way to the top but never succeeding, a ham-fisted metaphor so rooted in truth you almost felt stupid for not knowing earlier when you first understood.

Soon there were no more crabs to haul. The owner of the marina had enough of your luck and sternly asked that you both never come back to this dock to throw traps. Your dad smiled and said, "Sure thing, guy!" fully knowing there weren't any crabs left anyway. You carried your white plastic bucket of scuttling ocean spiders, pinching claws, tumbling shell-backed antennae eyes, desperate for life in confusion, and walked down Ocean County Road to 16th Street with your pops like you had been born upon the sea.

Now your dad is cooking them in the pebble backyard of the rental house. Your mother sits on the wooden picnic table, smoking a cigarette and reading *Vanity Fair*. It makes you uncomfortable to see the crabs being killed. You mostly just wanted to catch them, to keep them as pets, to be their friend. They look too much like bugs to be appetizing anyway. Now you watch the remaining cluster in the bucket, waiting to be cooked alive and served with butter, frantically thrashing on top of each other for an escape that could only succeed if they maintained the self-awareness to work as a team.

Your dad feeds you some meat to see if you like the taste. "Yuck! Tastes like caca!" you say, quoting a cartoon you saw on television that morning. Your father's smile sinks into a disgusted frown. He slaps you upside the head and pulls you by the ear, back toward the house.

"What did you say, dupa?"

"Nothing!"

"Where did you hear that?"

"I don't know! I don't know!"

He spanks you a few good times on the bum and sends you to stand facing the corner of the living room for 10 minutes while your mom watches through the window from the picnic table outside. Every so often you check behind you to see your dad cooking and your mother reading, acting as if you never existed. In this moment you couldn't care less to eat a crab. You wish to run out screaming, knock the bucket over and set the crabs free to crawl away into the pines. Maybe in a few hours they could make it to the ocean. The tears will dry from your eyes, but before they do, you are watching your father and mother laugh together without you, feeling like a king who fell from the grace of his throne.

* * *

You are in Beach Haven, the southernmost borough on Long Beach Island, staring at the spiraling chutes of the water park, sliding children in descending loops into the bright blue of an over-chlorinated pool. Kids are pulling levers that douse them in flash-flood showers. Others pump spray soaker guns, hoses cabled to playset turrets, to shoot down their enemies, their cousins, their sisters, their friends.

Beyond that, the Viking Ship of Fantasy Island Theme Park sways and saws back and forth like Poe's pendulum in the pit, while children scream and young fathers heartily laugh at their offspring's dismay. A caterpillar roller coaster chugs over bumps and tight corners. Teenagers shoot BB rifles at balloons in a stall to win their girlfriends cheap stuffed animal knockoffs of cartoon characters popular in bygone generations.

Behind you is a mini mall shaped vaguely like a ship. Mothers walk their daughters holding wire cages of hermit crabs with pattern-painted shells and a lifespan of maybe a week before they are neglected to the indignity of their flushed toilet grave. Brothers walk past the outdoor replica of an old brigantine, smacking each other's heads with the plastic of their toy pirate swords while their father unwraps the casing on sea green saltwater taffy, pops it in his mouth, and chews heavily with the candy stuck in the narrow crevices of his teeth.

You walk into the local homemade fudge shop, wait in line, and order. As the teenage girl cuts your fudge, she rolls her eyes to her coworker and says audibly, "Kill me now."

Her coworker nods in agreement.

You remember your first job and the feeling of defeat clocking in each day. You want to tell them not to worry because things will get better, and there will be better jobs, and better days, and the freedom of adulthood to enjoy, but you think of the factory, the bleakness of the repetition in the valves, the morning walk that once produced a calmness, a Zen within your soul, as the sun rose pumpkin orange over the truss of the rusted iron bridge before downtown, and all you can say to them as you receive your quarters in change is a quiet "Thank you," but she has already walked away.

* * *

You are biking around the back bay streets of Barnegat Light with a black patch strapped over your left eye and a Chicago White Sox baseball cap with a curved brim, worn slightly off-kilter upon your head. The day before, a strong wind blew grains of sand into your face and temporarily blinded you. You squealed, crying while your dad frantically drove you to the nearest eye doctor, where in a dark room they analyzed you with prodding tools and bright lights that made you see the whole spectrum of rainbow colors flashing across your vision like a psychedelic trip.

You feel tough now, pedaling your bicycle with an eyepatch, like a rogue street pirate, a lone wolf, with no parental supervision. The doctors and your mother made sure to mention how brave you had been. You have never felt stronger.

Toward the Viking Village Fish Market, your rabbit-ear-bowed shoelaces catch in the spiraling gears of your bicycle. The shoelaces wrap up like a coiled snake, snag, and send you scraped onto the side of the road with your Mongoose bike stuck on top of you. Pathetically, you cry for help. Nobody comes. The eyepatch isn't cool anymore. It makes it harder to attempt to escape.

You hear the sound of a car screeching to a stop. A van door slides open. "Are you okay, little boy?" a girl's voice calls out. You turn your head to see three high-school-aged girls walking up to you. One pulls out a pocket knife, kneels down, and cuts you free of your laces.

"Thank you, miss," you say to her, and she laughs.

"Are you lost, little guy? Do you need a ride?" You bashfully shake your head *no*.

"It's okay," another says. "We don't bite. We'll take you home to your mommy and daddy." You shake your head again, feeling the wetness in your shorts dribble down your leg.

"Well, you can't ride this thing," the third says. "It's all busted." She kicks it and smirks to herself.

"Come on, get in. Come with us," they say. You nod your head. One of them grips you by the hand and pulls you up, leading you into the middle-row seat of the van where she sits you on her lap.

The girl who cut your shoelaces off is driving in the wrong direction. You never told her where you live. You realize you don't know the actual address of where your parents are staying, and your heart sinks.

"Ew, he peed his pants when he fell," the girl whose lap you are on says as they all laugh.

"Aw! Well, take his shorts off then." You squirm while this girl pulls off your clothes and wipes you down with your own underwear. "Aren't you too old for that, kid?"

"Look at his little wiener!" says the girl next to you, giggling. She reaches out and wiggles your penis between her pointer finger and thumb. Your body freezes in shock and embarrassment, not knowing what to do. Older boys have talked to you about sexual encounters as enjoyable, as a status symbol. There's a tingling sensation inside of you, but more so you just want to go home. "I like your little eyepatch! Hah! Look it's getting bigger!"

"God, you're such a weirdo," the girl driving says. "Where do you live, little boy?"

The other girl is still stroking your now-hard genitals while the girl whose lap you are on holds you so you don't squirm. They are both laughing. "Oh my God, this is too funny!" they say to each other. You whimper and tense your legs.

"Where do you live, little boy?" the driver says again. You scrape the edges of your brain for a location but can only focus on the fear of the situation and the daunting memory of the girl in the movie theater, the pale horse of a woman moving in to give you a kiss.

"By the mustache!" You manage to yell. "Ah!" you wail as the girl has managed to stroke your prick enough to spout a few small drops of white onto back of the seat in front of you.

"Gross! He got it on the leather!"

"You're nasty! Come on, let's get rid of him."

"By the mustache?" asks the driver.

"The mustache restaurant!"

"Mustache Bill's?"

"Yes! Yes!" you shriek as tears flow down your face.

The van pulls a U-turn on Ocean County Road, and in the few minutes it takes to get to the diner, the girl whose lap you are on has put your clothes back on and used your own bare hand to wipe up the drops of white from the leather seat in front of you. Your palm is sticky, and you are afraid to touch anything with it.

In the parking lot of Mustache Bill's Diner, they toss you out the sliding side door of the van onto the pebble drive where you scrape your knees for the second time this day. "Sorry, kid!" the driver says. "God, you guys are just too funny. You're sick, you know that?"

"He should feel lucky to get some action with that little thing," one of the girls says.

Before you can get up and turn around, the door has slammed shut, and they have pulled out into traffic and sped away, honking. You remember their sharp laughter and razor smiles. You will never be able to remember their faces. For a few minutes, you sit in the parking lot of Mustache Bill's with a dark tan piss stain on the front of your khaki shorts and a sticky smear of white on the palm of your hand. Your White Sox hat fell off in the van. Your dad is going to be very angry you lost it.

You now feel very stupid wearing an eye patch. An older man asks if you are lost and offers to help you find your parents. You grunt and run away in the direction of home.

* * *

"Laaaaaadies and geeeentlemennnnn! Welcome to the Showplace Ice Cream Parlooooorrrrrr!" To a roar of applause, a young man with a red and white pinstripe vest, black bow tie, and headset microphone claps and skips out across the black and white checkered tile floor as another identical man carries out your ice cream sundae. "As you all know now, here at the Showplace, we sing for our food! Right here I have brought this little boy the 'Annie' sundae! So little boy, I'm going to have you sing for me—Tomorrow! Tomorrow! I'll diet tomorrow!"

The room is in an expectant silence. With your one not-patched eye, you look down to your strawberry ice cream topped with strawberries, marshmallows, banana wheels, whipped cream, and a maraschino cherry in a clamshell-shaped ceramic white bowl, wishing this man would leave you alone so you can eat in peace. "Come on, hon," your mother urges you. You look to her, then your server, and shake your head.

"Let's hear it, buddy—Tomorrow! Tomorrow! I'll diet tomorrow!" he sings louder.

"C'mon, boy. Sing!" your father says, smacking your shoulder.

"I don't want to!" you say, avoiding eye contact.

"Everybody has to sing for their food!" the server says. "C'mon, guys! Sing! Sing! Sing!"

The whole room is chanting, "Sing!" to you now while you try not to cry. You still haven't told anyone what happened to you earlier, though your father did question the stain of your khakis and the missing White Sox hat. He even made you walk alone, all the way back to grab your bike. The crowd draws quiet again, waiting for your next move. As a few soft tears roll down your cheek, you croon, almost in a whisper, "Tomorrow...tomorrow...I'll diet.... tomorrow...." The audience roars in applause.

"Why you cryin', boy?" Your father slaps your shoulder again.

"That looks good! Can I get a bite?" your mother says, scooping a lump of pink ice cream with your spoon. She swallows a mouthful, then reaches out with her other hand and wipes your cheeks with a napkin. "Here, dry your eyes, baby. It wasn't so bad, all you had to do was sing. It's over now!"

A recording of a pipe organ plays over the PA, while another server in a pinstripe vest and bowtie dashes out onto the floor with a black cape and an off-white, pointy-nosed mask. "The phantooooom of the showplaaaace is here!" he sings while children and their parents everywhere around you laugh and clap.

* * *

"What's this photo?" your wife asks, thumbing through an old set of disposable camera prints in a drawer. "I've never seen it before." She holds the 4x6 up to show the lens-flared image of you as a young boy, standing on a pebble driveway with a squirt gun, smiling, a black patch strapped over one eye.

"Oh, that's me at the Jersey Shore. I used to go there as a kid."

"What happened to your eye?"

"Got scratched with sand in a wind storm."

"You look so happy! We should go there again sometime! I wanna see where you used to travel to when you were a kid."

"Eh, I don't know ..."

"C'mon, let's go! It's gotta be cathartic to go back to a place like that."

"Well, sure. Yeah, maybe this summer."

"Let's do it!"

"Allright. Gotta go to work, boo. I'll see you in the morning."

"See ya, baby."

You slip your arms through your denim jacket, kiss your wife with a peck on the lips, and exit out the back door down the wooden stoop toward the yellow track lights of the Red Line in the purple dusk. From your kitchen, your dog barks a muffled goodbye.

* * *

It is your family's last day on the Jersey Shore, and your father has decided to spend some quality time with his son. You watched as he bartered with the leather-faced fishermen of the marina to rent a motorized dinghy and some fishing rods to putt out across the back bay and catch something to gut and grill for dinner. The weathered fishermen were not impressed by his big-city antics, and your father was not intimidated by their stoic faces and dismissive gestures.

"Alright, Captain Ahab!" your father croaked, reluctantly handing them the full amount in cash. The man said nothing. Sneering, he grabbed the bills, puffed a black cloud of pipe smoke from the side of his mouth, and walked away into the clutter of his shop.

Now your father steers the purring motor of the dinghy across the rolling hills of evergreen waves. He prepares the lines of the fishing rods and gets annoyed with you when you don't want to touch the squirming purple worms to pierce and hook them on as bait. Once in your childhood, your father sat you down and made you watch *The Old Man and the Sea* on the Turner Classic Movies channel. You had no idea a sunset's colors could bleed as stark above a fishing boat in real life as they did in Technicolor.

You are so excited to catch your first fish that neither you nor your father notice the dinghy putting past the lighthouse on the inlet that you have only ever viewed from land. The fish is ugly, discolored, and flat. Its eyes are smushed together on one side like how a child would draw a face without any sense of dimensions.

"Ah, it's a fucking flounder!" your father groans. He holds the fish by the hook stuck through its bloody mouth, and wiggles it at you, mimicking its woman's voice. "Chodź tutaj, daj mi buzi, kochanie!" He jokes in Polish, pretending the wide-eyed fish is asking you to give it a kiss. With pinched fingers, he loops the hook out of the flounder's lips and tosses it, flapping desperately, into the gleaming rays of sunset, splashing back into the sea.

"Holy smokes! We're out there, Boo Boo!" your father says, pointing to the shoreline, which is much more distant and smaller than you remember it being moments before. Your dinghy is out in open water. The people lounging on the beach are the size of sand fleas now. Your father's boat feels too small to float freely in such depths during the oncoming darkness. "Better give this thing a break!" He laughs nervously, turning off the sputtering motor. "Don't want it to run out of fuel!"

"Dad? Are we gonna be okay? I mean, are we supposed to be out here?" As the seconds pass, the ocean currents are drawing you farther out into the endless green.

"Of course, Boo Boo Bear! What? You don't trust your father? Fine! Have it your way! I'll get this motor going again, and we'll head back around the bend, really check out Old Barney! When we tell your mother, she's gonna get a kick out of this!" It is now hard to see the shoreline over the arc of the waves and the sinking of the anchor sun. The motor pouts and sputters a few times while your father rips the chain, cursing under his breath. He tells you everything is going to be all right. You adjust the strap of your eyepatch around your head. You don't believe him.

* * *

"I'm going back to Jersey," you tell Aulina, cruising Lakeshore Drive in her car. "You might not see me for a bit."

"What if you don't see *me*?" She laughs. "What if one day you crawl back for more and I'm long gone? That's your problem. You come and go and drift far away, and you don't realize that sometimes when you create that distance, the closeness you had is dead."

"Aw, c'mon. That's spontaneity! That's living life!"

"You've always been one foot in and one foot out. Not just with me. Everything. You've been spontaneous. You've taken risks. But you've never taken the truest risk. That's commitment. Life didn't fail you. You failed yourself."

You ride together in silence to the North Side to grab dinner. You are so immersed in watching the waves of Lake Michigan out the passenger window that when you turn back you are surprised to see Aulina is crying.

* * *

A dead whale is stranded in the wash of the shallows, jaw unhinged from its head, exposing lines of rigid teeth. Its body is a scraped blue, gray, and cardinal red, swaddled in the white foam of the breakers. You watch it from a distance, sure you are the only one on the beach. How? Why today? The one morning the beach is empty. Your last day here. It's slumped there like a slain dragon, a dinosaur sunk in tar. You have now seen one of earth's most magnificent creations struck down by the backhanded slap of hooded death.

"Better not get any closer!" a gruff voice says.

You turn to see an old fisherman, his face bronzed and wrinkled with age, peppered hair gray and white as the spray of the waves. Black smoke puffs from a pipe clung to the corner of his mouth. You recall the man your father once chartered a dinghy from and quickly try to calculate the years gone by.

"Someone's gotta do something!"

"Yes, yes. Before the tide comes in. Look." He points beyond the whale. "You can already see the scavengers." You stare harder and are able to pick out the fins circling off the coast, waiting for their chance with the rise of the waters.

"Who are we supposed to call?"

"I already called the town."

"Can they help it?"

"It's already dead, son. See, most whales die in a whale fall. Out in deep water. Bathyal or abyssal zones. A dead whale out there can feed the critters on the ocean floor for a few tens of years, I suppose. Creates a whole ecosystem. Dyin' here does the ocean no good. The sharks'll get it with the high tide. If it don't explode."

"Why would it explode?"

"You smell that smell?'

"I think so?"

"That's not the ocean, son. That's the gasses of the blubber. When the whale decomposes, it goes through putrefaction. Its tissue breaks down and makes gasses, methane, and such. The fermentation produces carbon dioxide. When the fermentation and the putrefaction come together, the whale bloats real big. See how it is over there, all bloated? That's the gas trapped in the blubber, boy! And trapped gas has to eventually explode."

"You seen one do that before?"

"That's why I said don't get closer. Its intestines'll burst 30 to 50 feet into the air. Don't wanna stand under it, get my drift?"

"But what's the town gonna do?"

"They gotta hire a boat and drag it out to the open water. Out there they gotta be real careful to cut it open and let out the gas. If they can do that, it'll sink down, create a whale fall, like I told you usually happens out there."

"Well, what if they cut it wrong?"

"Then *poof!* There's intestines flying like seabirds, boy."

"So where are they gonna get the boat?"

"Why, me! That's what I do! I charter boats!" The fisherman lets out a hearty laugh and grips your shoulder. Together you watch the gargantuan dead whale, bloated fat with fuming gasses that stink rotten across the ocean air. Eventually, town officials show up. The fisherman is happy to lend his services, for a price.

Before you know it, you have been at the beach into the afternoon. High tide is coming. The town has issued a "no swim" ordinance. The old fisherman who you have convinced yourself you met in the misadventures of your childhood is now steering a ship, hauling the whale out of the shallows, past the oncoming scavenging sharks. There is a red hue to the water in its wake. You feel as if you have witnessed something holy. An obscure holiness, unbeknownst to most men. Or even priests. You watch until the whale is towed off into the unseeable distance. You hardly noticed the crowd forming around you on the heat of the afternoon sands. Your eyes only see the whale and the weathered face of the fisherman, stoic in determination. Smoke curls from his pipe. His dedication to the sea is boundless. Reverent. Devout.

ULICZNY OPRYSZEK

"Mama! Papa is sleeping in the air!"

When they cut him down, they never truly removed the noose from the tree branch on which he swayed. Every glance out the back window was a concrete reminder of the way he chose to leave. The crisp bonfire scent of the scarlet Chicago fall faded into bitter frost and glacial snow, and still the tether's remnants remained. It was easier to close the blinds. To turn up the radio. Turn on the TV. To pray. But soon you lost faith in God's plan. Prayers went unanswered. You decided that the will of God was in the rope. And you grew callous.

"Listen," your mother told you, "It's you and me now. We are a team. You're all I got, little boy! You are like North Star to me. And I will be like North Star to you!"

"Sure, Mom," you told her. But you couldn't comprehend how a guiding light like her would let your father leave in such a way.

The day you cut the rope down was the day of your first fight in school. You had always succumbed to bullying, on the bus, on the block, in the classroom. It was easier to take the punch, receive the spit, turn the cheek to harsh words, cry into the pillow in the middle of the night. Over the years it made you nauseous with anxiety, bloated with the toxicity of your antagonizing peers. Then one day without warning your fist thrust across a young boy's face in the lunchroom, sending his glasses in the air, shattering on the tile floor. You hardly recall making the decision to do so. Maybe it was fate. Either way, when you got home you faced the noose, slashed it down with a kitchen knife, and tossed it into the alley dumpster.

"Dziękuję, kochanie," your mother said to you, opening the window blinds to the spring's fertile bloom. "Your father seen many rough times in life. In the steel plants, poverty, a youth under Communism. Left his family behind and never saw them again. His face was so serious, but in his heart was much sorrow. In old age his ghosts now caught up to him." The sun's yolk ran into the robin's egg sky above the birth of green lawns and pastel flowers. Your mother hugged you tight and kissed your forehead. You felt a strength grow inside you from your actions in school that day. It was then that you embraced the power and redemption obtained through violence.

* * *

You are in your bedroom assembling a Lego tower on a beige rug. It stands about a foot high, rigid and misshapen, in no specific color coordination. Different plastic knights in war helmets and painted armor hold tiny swords, daggers, spears, and crossbows. There is a random chef character mixed in to the army from another box set. He is holding a miniature spoon, though within his dimensions it is probably the size of a broom.

The previous week, an acquaintance from school came over to play. Naturally, you brought out your Lego sets and toy soldiers, ready to imagine yourselves as devastating gods of war, overseeing dramatic legacies with humorous slapstick twists. In one moment a general would brutally decapitate an archer with a broadsword, in another he would be sent shooting up into the ceiling of the room by your hands, powered by his own farts, like a geyser. If war was hell, it could also be a sick, sick joke.

Your acquaintance did not want to play though. In fact, when you dug your Tupperware of Lego characters out of the closet, he said words to you that you didn't yet understand, though you knew them to be harmful. Then, "You still play with toys?" he asked, and with a red face, you knew your reputation at school would take a dive for quite some time.

You came up with cheap excuses that he didn't believe. It seemed you both felt that you owed him an explanation. The rest of the day the boy smiled and laughed but not with you. By the time he left, your eagerness to please and entertain had ceased, and all you were left with was a deep unshakable shame that made you curse your residual imagination. The boys around you strived to settle into reality. You wanted to play, and you knew it to be wrong.

You put the finishing touch on your Lego tower. It is comically tall and thin, at this point almost up to two feet. A few weeks ago, you would beam with pride. You are chasing that high. Now you pout. It isn't the same. Your iron gauntlet sweeps through the plastic castle and tumbles the building blocks of your creation across the frayed strands of the beige rug. You rip apart the connecting pieces and toss them around the room in a huff. "So stupid..." you say to yourself. From the floor, the chef character, out of place in this medieval horde, looks up to you with round black eyes, holding that stupid plastic spoon, almost the length of his entire body.

* * *

You are inside the single-stall men's bathroom of a late-night dive bar on North Avenue while industrial music and death rock pulses over the speakers at such a high volume that it is impossible to hold a conversation without yelling. Outside the bathroom, amateur strippers dance on the steel bar top in short skirts and platform shoes or heels, under dim chandeliers strung up with hanging bras and panties that quite possibly have been there since the 1990s. Bearded bartenders with bald heads take bitter grapefruit shots of Malört and eye the pushed-up cleavage of their female counterparts, their curved skin exposed from doctored heavy metal t shirts in a uniform of solid black.

The walls, mirror, sink, and toilet of the bathroom are covered in metal band, bar, and clothing brand stickers, most faded and torn, some half peeled off intentionally by drunken rivals of scenesters, their hate magnified by the influence of alcohol and pills. You and your boys are crowded around the sink, shouting over each other's opinions to get your voice in while your heart races and a friend pulls out a bag of white powder.

"You guys know Two Dollar Eddie?"

"What the fuck kinda name is Two Dolla—"

"Hey, shut up! Shut up! I'm talking!"

"Fuck him anyway!"

"It's a stupid name!"

"You don't even know why they call him that—"

"That's the story!"

"C'mon, let'm talk!"

"Okay ..."

"So shut up then!"

"Jeeeesus Christ ..."

"What was I sayin'?"

"Two Dollar Eddie!"

"Right! So, Two Dollar Eddie does anything for two bucks. You gotta give it to him up front of course, but anything you dare him to do, he does it. They say he licked the floor of this bathroom from the doorway up to the toilet bowl once for eight quarters."

"Nah!"

"There's a video of it somewhere!"

"Prolly got AIDS now honestly ..."

"At least herpes."

"Maybe hepatitis ..."

"Hey, fuck you, jagoffs, let's snort some toot."

"You're just mad cause you got hepatitis!"

"Nah, dude, it was gonorrhea, and that shit's curable!"

"Whatever ..."

"Some dirty broads out there, dude!"

"Fuck you, give me a bump!"

Your friend hands you the bag of cocaine, and with the smile of a little boy opening a cookie jar, you pull out a miniature plastic spoon and dip it in for a tiny scoop of powder. Your friends are all laughing hysterically. "You guys like that?" you say to them, sniffing the blow up your left nostril from the toy. "Got it off an old Lego set. Who knew it would still be fun to play with that shit?"

"Let me try!" says a friend. He grabs it, scoops, and snorts a bump too.

Your group pours out of the bathroom into the barroom where a long line has formed. They stare at you like they will beat your ass. Their eyes are wide and red, pupils dilated just like yours. Your group stares back at them like you all can beat their ass too. Some curses are mouthed under everyone's breath. Instead of fighting, the men in line crowd the bathroom to engage in the same ritual they got mad at you for taking part in. No one likes to wait.

Your go to the boxing machine. It's in the corner by a metal pole, stretching from floor to ceiling, that a voluptuous young woman is lazily dancing on and flipping her hair around. You and your friends take turns putting dollars in the machine, reeling your arms back and throwing haymakers into the retractable red punching bag to see how the arcade game rates the strength of your fists. You are all shouting over each other more incoherently now, sending sidelong horny glances to the wiggling girl on the pole, looking more blatantly than you are aware of. Your upper jaw is shifting left while your lower jaw is shifting right. The wiggle of your nose and movement of your lips are uncontrollable. It is starting to creep out the women around you.

"Love that fucking spoon, Spider! Good form!"

"Isn't that shit hilarious?" you say, slurring your words. Another friend has turned the punching game into a joke and is head butting the bag with the thick of his tattooed forehead as the people around him either shake their heads in embarrassment or point and laugh. You hardly process what is going on around you right now. You are too busy remembering that day the boy came over to play and changed the way you acted forever.

* * *

"I bet you're a virgin anyway!"

"You're just jealous mine's a little bigger!"

You are on a yellow school bus headed from Archer Heights to the Brookfield Zoo in the Chicagoland suburbs.

The boys in the seats around you are all measuring each other's penises while the middle-aged woman chaperone in the front seat turns a blind eye to avoid addressing the situation. Girls in your section of the bus are sneaking peeps, not so discretely. Some boys blush and swipe at them to go away, while others proudly display their maturing bodies.

The boy across the aisle from you has never liked you. He has been giving you a hard time for years.

"You're still gonna be a virgin even when your 50 years old!" Everyone laughs at his comment.

"I'm actually not a virgin, dipshit!" You state this proudly, gaining the interest of your inexperienced peers.

"Oh yeah? Who was he?" They all laugh, then settle down to receive the juicy gossip.

"Lost it to three high school girls in New Jersey when I graduated fifth grade!"

"No shit ..." The boy has a newfound respect for you. The guys around you slap high fives and pat your back. You are now the biggest player they know. It is as if they have all forgotten that you play with kids' toys in your room after school lets out.

"How? How did it happen?" one boy says. "What was it like?" You notice the girls around the other rows of seats looking at you with a newfound wonder, almost a sense of envy.

"Well, I didn't have to do nothin' ..." you say. "They came to me ..." You begin to tell a skewed story of the day you were picked up in a van with pissed shorts and tears in your eyes on the Jersey Shore. It isn't the story of a boy who cried himself to sleep for days, maybe even weeks after, who could never tell his own father, mother, or closest friends, who became scared of sex and women for years, who waited long after most others to lose his virginity because of unseen marks in his heart and mind. In this story you are the hero. You are an alpha man, a magnet for soaked pussies and ripe girls in bikinis, driving vans around the beach in search of a boy like you that they could have entirely for themselves.

Your story is more interesting to them than the prospect of encaged jungle animals pacing back and forth in their shoddy enclosures. You walk off the steps of the bus into the sunlight and enter the arching gates of the Brookfield Zoo feeling like the biggest lying chump there ever was.

* * *

You are standing at the entrance of your high school at the end of the day, waiting for the bus. A classmate you recognize as Beto is walking past the flagpole on the sidewalk when six older kids appear from the ether and beat him down to the ground with their fists, then proceed to stomp him with their feet. In response, other boys jump into the fray and attempt to tear Beto's attackers off. You are frozen in a panic, watching the mass of thrashing bodies, and hardly notice an older guy who doesn't go to your school walking up to the mesh of fists with his right hand in the side pocket of his blue jeans.

Screams sound out from the front yard of the school. Desperate cries of onlooking girls and grunts and wails of boys being beaten. The oncoming stranger pulls his hand from his pocket, and the grunts of the boys turn into shrieking feminine bays as he stabs his way to the center of the brawl, plunging his knife into the ribs of Beto's attackers and saviors alike.

His knife is washed in claret. Schoolyard thugs are writhing on the ground, holding their stomachs, sides, and thighs, parting like a biblical ocean as the man to be known as Beto's cousin drags him off the concrete, bleeding from his ears and nose. They are walking fast, then jogging, then Beto is forced to sprint, leaving his backpack behind. Sirens howl like whizzing bullets toward you across the cool of the mid-autumn air as the rubber of tires burns out on the battered body of Beto's cousin's rusted off-white Coupe de Ville.

* * *

Your mother has always told you that the blasting sounds you hear year-round in the middle of the night are the Mexicans celebrating with their fireworks that they drive to Indiana to buy. You have always wondered why the Mexicans love fireworks so much and why they have so many holidays to celebrate.

This perception has changed now that you are watching a car pull up to the side of a local taqueria while your mother takes you out for ice cream. A fist bursts out the rolled-down window holding a black pistol and fires a bullet with the pop of a firework into the chest of a 15-year-old kid, walking his girlfriend down the street from their date night, holding their school bags on their backs.

You drop your ice cream cone in a melted green lump on the ground. The chocolate chips scatter the fallen scoop like bullet holes. The slain boy crumples to the concrete. His girlfriend is in hysterics, weeping over his body, thrashing her arms and kicking violently on the sidewalk. The vehicle careens away with a purr, a pop, and a roar. Your mother drags you around the corner by your arm. You whimper because it hurts, staring back over your shoulder at the sight of your first dead body. You now know there is nothing to celebrate in life. Love has left the neighborhood.

* * *

Nineteenth Street and Kedzie, North Lawndale. The house you are in looks like a bomb went off. Trap music blasts from pawn shop speakers balanced on a rickety wooden coffee table, leveled with coasters layered under one of the legs. The room is clouded in the stench of rancid smoke. A TV is on, but the sound is not audible, and you can barely see the image on the screen, just the flashes of bright lights reflected in the misty gloom. The counters are covered in ashes of cigarettes, cans of beer, empty handles of booze, week-old food, and the occasional crawling bug. The couches are lined with users lighting up or passed out in euphoria. Through the walls somewhere, a baby shrieks muffled cries.

A mangy brown dog with a baseball sized tumor on its ribs runs through the hall with a rope in its teeth in search of a playmate, claws clicking on the linoleum tile floor. There is an abrasion on its face that wets its fur with blood. You didn't notice until you reached out and pet it. Now your fingers are smeared with rouge. You shake your head out of your buzzed trance to see an acquaintance talking to you, holding a pipe and a lighter. You wipe your hand on your pants and try and focus your eyes to reinsert yourself into the conversation.

"It's all chill, bro, don't be nervous, it's your first time, know what I'm sayin'? This shit is like … it's like when you breathe this in, you breathin' in all the bad shit in your life. All that fucked up shit you been through. But when you breathe out, fam, you breathin' out fuckin' everything. I mean everything. It's all gone."

"But it don't last long, right?"

"Bet. The euphoria, maybe 15 to 20 seconds. Best of your life. Then it's just a normal high. Y'all will be geeked as fuck, dude. Shit's better than sex."

He breathes in and out with closed eyes and a sigh of deep satisfaction. It is a while before he truly opens his eyes and hands the pipe to you. You reach out to take it and reel your hand back in surprise.

"Pipe's hot, Spider. Look at my lips. I got blisters, bitch! Shit's no joke! First time I smoked dis shit, the heat cracked my back molar in half. When I breathed out, I spit out half the tooth into my hand. Got no insurance so just left it like that. Shit, that shit got so infected it hurt to touch, or even drink water, much less hard liquor and beer. Girls didn't wanna kiss me when we fucked cause it smelled like rot when I opened my mouth. Finally caved and went to a dentist. When he touched my cheek, it hurt so bad I almost lit him up from the fuckin' chair. He was like 'Hooooly shit! I've never seen a tooth this bad in all my 20 years in practice.' Mothafucka looked like he was gonna spew, bitch ass. But don't worry, bro, that ain't gonna happen to you. That's why I'm tellin' you to watch yo-self in advance. So you don't wind up like me, missin' teeth and shit. Here, use my lighter."

You put that crack pipe to your lips and feel the burning sensation and the thick warmth of the smoke entering your mouth. It is like this man said. You breathe in the weight of the world and blow out a full-body sensation so powerful it seems heaven sent. It is a sensation so fulfilling you already know you will never feel anything like it again for the rest of your life.

* * *

It is the first Monday of March, Casimir Pulaski day in Chicago. Your mother has taken you out of middle school early to go to a local parade. Cars crawl by with banners written in the old language from the Polish Roman Catholic Union and the Polish Museum of America. Fair haired women march in dresses of red and white, while men dress in red caps pricked with long feathers, hand-stitched overcoats, and red ribbons around the collar of their white shirts tucked under blue patterned vests. They are costumed as traditional Eastern Krakowians. The older Poles smile and wave, and the younger trudge along, pouting, having been forced to dress up for the occasion.

"Kazimierz Pułaski was a Polish cavalry officer who fought for America in the Revolution," your mother tells you. "When Poles first immigrated here, 'za chlebem', they faced discrimination. So, to prove they were Americans, they made Pułaski a hero."

"You tell me every year, Mom."

"I like telling you." She smiles.

She goes up to a vendor and purchases you a pączki. You push your way through the crowd and plant your ass on the curb of the sidewalk looking out into the street. The parade briefly stops as a waltz-like piano plays over some speakers, and a group of dancers perform to a brief mazurka.

The dance ends, and the parade marches on to claps, whistles, and cheers. People wave red and white flags of the old country as a brass band steps up, playing a polka. You walk away. The horns sound like someone taking a crap. You swallow your last bit of doughnut and wipe your mouth on your sleeve.

You make your way back through the crowd, searching for your mother. You call her name, but your voice is drowned out under the music and cheering. You lick your powdered fingers, then wipe what's left on your pants. That's when you see your mother in the arms of a man over by the pączki vendor. You have not seen her with a man since your father passed. He rubs her lower back in a circular, soothing motion that infuriates you.

You want to run up and punch this man in the balls for his audacity. You will not allow your mother to be with anyone else. Out of respect for your father's love. In your eyes, she must remain untouched for the rest of her days. The crapping of the brass horns mixed with this startling image is enough to drive you mad. His hands won't stop caressing her. He reaches high and low. She turns and smiles to him. You never see his face.

You want to fight. You want to kill. You ball your fingers into a fist, but all you can do is cry. And you run. You run all the way home and leave your mother there at the parade with this man. You punch into your bed pillows and curse her as a whore.

* * *

Mariusz Wojciech was the son of a firefighter. They lived off 57th and Narragansett down the street from John F. Kennedy High School out by Midway. Mid-June every year, you and your friends would stop by the Wojciechs' single-car garage to gawk at the homemade 10-inch mortars Mariusz peddled to the neighborhood kids for a reasonable price. Mariusz's father ran the local Fourth of July fireworks display.

With the help of some of the other firefighters, Mr. Wojciech would post up his rockets and mortars in Wentworth Park and set the sky alight with cracking neon fizzling into trickling ashes and smoldering embers draped like boughs of willow trees above crowds with plastic beer cups on striped picnic blankets and burning sausages on round charcoal grills. You could only imagine what the passengers on the flights from Midway Airport saw below them as they traveled up and west out of the city to somewhere far away. Someday, when you had money, you promised yourself you would book a ticket and take that flight.

That flight never came. The fireworks ended abruptly one summer when a boy who had snuck into his father's cooler of Old Style ran up to Mariusz as the son of the head firefighter was about to light off one last explosive. He kicked his legs to punt the 10-inch mortar into the air like a football. Mariusz's stoic face lit animated in surprise. All he could do was dive out of the way as the drunken boy's foot connected to the mortar and blew clean off in the last legal firework explosion heard around the neighborhood for years to come.

From there, all you remember is hearing the sounds of screams and sirens. Mariusz and the drunken boy heard nothing. The explosion quaked their ears stone deaf. The boy was transported to Mercy Hospital in an ambulance where he stayed for quite some time.

When you saw him again, a stainless-steel prosthetic protruded from a stump below his knee and tucked snug into the faded white tongue of his New Balance tennis shoe. He couldn't look anyone at school in the eyes, not that they were looking at his eyes. Wherever he went, all the kids stared at his deformity, the mark of his stupidity, and found a good enough reason to keep the boy on the outside of their social circles.

You are in the Wojciechs' garage now for the first time in a couple years since the incident. Mariusz is sitting on a milk crate in the corner smoking a clove cigarette and drinking a 40-ounce of Baltika Malt Liquor. *I wish I was single. My pockets would jingle. I wish I was single again...* His father's "Mały Władziu" polka records, of Li'l Wally, the Polka King, are playing on an old turntable. Mariusz cannot hear a note. When he sees you and your friends, you are certain he recognizes you, but his head nod is so slight it seems he is not acknowledging anything at all. He removes his cigarette in pinched fingers, spits on the ground, then returns it to his lips in something of a sneer. You avert your eyes.

Mr. Wojciech hands you a case of Baltika and a box of Roman candles, and in return, you hand him the wad of cash that your friends pooled from wherever you could find the dough. You and your boys joke and smile, clinking bottles together and running out into the street with your shoddy box of explosive objects. Behind you, Mariusz gets up from his milk crate, clove smoke swimming as a translucent jellyfish off his down-curved lips. He reaches up to the handle and rips down the garage door in a rickety slide and bang onto the concrete, silencing the bouncing polka's accordions in a single motion.

You are running up Narragansett Avenue toward Archer Ave. and the high school, shooting off the Roman candles at each other's asses between swigs of cheap booze. The rockets bounce off the back curves of your jeans and careen into the street where they explode as you scream. Your friend finishes a Baltika and smashes the bottle on the hood of a car. The alarm sounds off. You all laugh and continue running. A man opens a second-story window and yells down at you. Another friend shoots a Roman candle that explodes in the air above this man's roof. He dives back into his room and eventually slams the window shut.

At Potok and Sons' Bakery you stop to use the bathroom. On your way in, you see a familiar face walking out. It is the boy whose foot was blown off by the firework just a few summers ago. He pays no mind to you as your eyes follow him down the street. You wave to the bakery clerk and enter the bathroom, only catching a glance out the window to see your friends calling over the deaf boy with their hands.

When you open the door to exit the bathroom, the boy is standing there in front of you smiling, holding a Roman candle that he is getting ready to set off. It lights and rockets towards you, barely missing your head, and ricochets around the bathroom stall. In a panic, you dive straight through this boy's body, knocking him off the balance of his prosthetic foot and tackling him to the ground. The candle explodes the plaster of the toilet and sends brown septic water fountaining across the room.

You scramble like a rat and burst out the doors of the bakery onto Archer Avenue to catch up with your friends who are already sprinting away toward an alley. Sirens are approaching down the block. Some-one has phoned the police. You never see the one-footed boy again after that. You imagine he was arrested but out of anxiousness feel no inclination to check the police report in the papers. Your boys later tell you about how they motioned him down and convinced him to shoot the rocket at you in the bathroom. How eager he was to finally make a group of friends.

* * *

It is Valentine's Day in middle school, and one of your teachers has assigned the class to write anonymous compliments for each student to be mixed in a brown paper bag for them to read. Some students groan, others flush red in embarrassment. You receive a pile of scrap paper and begin writing generic compliments to the people around you, not really taking time to put in much effort. When the teacher sorts the compliment cards and hands each bag to each individual student, there is a newfound eagerness within the classroom.

You shuffle through your cards. *You're cute,* reads one in girly, looping handwriting. *Go fuck yourself, puto. Nah, you alright,* reads another that you crumple up and flick off the edge of your desk. Perhaps the card that sticks out to you most, maybe for its authenticity, reads, *I think you have nice taste in t-shirts.*

You look down at your t-shirt, pinching the orange fabric with your fingers to stretch out the graphic in front of yourself. It is an AND1 basketball t-shirt with a faceless muscular man shaded gray in blue basketball shorts and gym shoes, crossing a white and gray basketball through his legs. *My game and yo mama,* it reads. *They both phat!* You don't really know what this means, but you've worn it to church some Sundays and received glares from some of the better dressed members of the congregation.

When the bell rings for the end of class, you all shuffle out the door. "Hey!" a girl calls out to stop you. It is Norma, the nerdiest girl in class. Her hair is long and frizzy. She wears a green thrift store fleece jacket covered in white and orange cat hair. Her eyes are large behind the thick frames of her taped-together glasses. In an attempt to dress up for Valentine's Day, she has tied a red ribbon on top of her head. Despite all these qualities, there is something about her that you genuinely think is adorable.

"Hey, what's up?" you ask. She is holding her schoolbooks and Lisa Frank Trapper Keepers tight to her chest, shifting her legs in nervousness.

"I just wanted to say," she tells you, averting her eyes, "I think you have really nice taste in shirts." People around you that hear start joking and laughing. You can tell she is uncomfortable, and you are too. You feel pressured to say something. The memories of the van full of girls on the Jersey Shore play back in your head, and you decide right then and there that you still cannot trust girls who supposedly have good intentions. And you don't know when you will be able to.

"Uh, cool ..." you say to Norma. You turn and walk away while people laugh at her rejection. Your guts churn inside. You know what you were supposed to say and do, but you couldn't do it, and you feel like less of a man for not doing so. But there is a mental block there. And in this moment walking down the crowded hall at the end of the school day, you decide it would be better to avoid the world of girl-friends, love, and sex entirely than it would be to face that black hole growing in your heart from a day you still never found the strength to talk about to your parents, much less your peers.

* * *

You and your buddy Michał are standing in the shadows of the highway underpass outside of Soldier Field, wearing blue and orange Bears jerseys over white Under Armour long sleeve shirts. Slunk on your heads are blue Bears beanies with orange C logos embroidered on the front fold. On your feet are tan Carhartt steel-toe boots, loosely laced. You have just witnessed the home team decimate the Detroit Lions. Brian Urlacher continuously barreled through Detroit's offensive line, forcing fumbles, making brutal tackles, paving the way for a Chicago victory.

There was a group of Detroit fans in the seats near you that you just couldn't get along with. What started as playful competitive jabs turned to full on smack talk, and when Detroit finally made a touchdown, one of the four fans in front of you swung his plastic cup of lager around in the air, swirling Miller Lite in an abrasive spray right into your eyes and mouth. In response, you and Michał chucked your beers at the back of his head, which resulted in the four Detroit fans charging you over the seat. The scuffle was quickly subdued by security, but no one involved could let it go that easily.

Now you see the four Lions fans approaching the underpass to head up the pathway to the Waldron parking lot deck. "Go back to Detroit, you fuckin' jagoffs!" you and your buddy yell and burst out of the shadows with your fists in the air. Michał strikes one fan across the face, and he stumbles and trips back onto the concrete. You dive and tackle another Detroit fan onto the ground where you start cross pummeling his nose into a bloody mess with your elbows. You only stop when another one of the four men rips you off his friend and slams you to the cement.

Michał is fighting two men at once, keeping them at a distance with reckless haymakers that sometimes land and sometimes swipe the air. One man charges him and is met with an uppercut that knocks him back. The other seizes the opportunity to jump in for the tackle, and your friend and this Lions fan are wrestling on the ground.

You are grappling with the man that slammed you to the concrete, while the fan you pounced on is writhing, holding his nose that runs red like a faucet. Your clothes are caked in dirt, blood, and sweat. You and Michał have your opponents planted below your knees by the time the hired Monterrey security staff comes to rip you away. You make sure to get in a few solid kicks to the ribs with your Carhartt boots, not noticing the crowd forming around you. "Fuck Detroit!" you spit behind you to reassert your sense of pride while you are escorted to the nearest police cruiser.

* * *

It is morning. You have been bailed out of jail by your mother. She pulls you by your ear and shoves you toward her car. When you both get in, she slaps you upside the head. You wince and grab your skull. "Why do you do this to your poor mother, eh?" she asks. You smile at her, and she tries her best not to smile back because she is still angry. "Jesteś ulicznym opryszek..." she says, calling you a "street ruffian," a "hoodlum," or a "street thug." Your Polish is very bad because you never tried too hard to learn and your parents were insistent that you grow up to be American, but you vaguely understand and you smile wider at her, beaming now with pride to be a brawny Chicagoan, the broad-shouldered kind that worries mothers and scares outsiders, the kind that eats meat and potatoes and drinks cheap pilsners, and smokes cigarettes on brick wall corners like a gutter vulture waiting to swoop in on the weak in the streets where only the strong survive.

"You should've seen him, man!" Michał tells your friends over Żywiec at the Karolinka Club. "He pounced on that asshole like a spider on a fly! Started smacking him upside the face with those elbows. For real, he looked like a spider on top of him."

"There you go!" says another. "That's what we'll call you now!"

"What's that?" you say, grinning in anticipation.

"Spider! That's your new nickname."

"I've had worse ..."

"To Spider!" Michał says. You clink your glasses and drink deep, the gleaming lights of the bar reflecting your face's image in the golden haze of your beer.

* * *

Nobody told you how horny the crack would make you. You stumble through the mist of the house party, struggling to maintain a set of open eyes. The thump of the music is disorienting. Before you know it, you have sunk into the leather of a tan beat-up couch and are staring at the sleeping body of a dark curvaceous woman whose long hair is done up in braids.

Your eyes are fading in and out. You watch her breasts rise up and down in her white tube top as she unconsciously breathes. The voices around you have disintegrated into the farting slides of trombones. The bloody tumorous dog jocks your leg, panting and wagging its tail. You kick it away, and it whimpers. The woman's lips are thick and painted smooth with red. You approach like a moth to a streetlight. You can't tell for sure, but it seems she is mouthing your name. "Spider ... Spider ... come here, baby."

Now you are lying in a field of white flowers in the heights of a

Carpathian mountainside. The spring sun watches you coyly behind the drifting clouds. The jaunty sawing strings of violins and cellos screech over the discordant bellowing chorus of the Goral people, the Polish Highlanders singing falsettos in gwara. Muzyka góralska. You can almost see their circular black-brimmed hats pierced with white feathers, their sheepskin waistcoats fastened with thick leather belts, the woolen outer coats worn like capes over their white linen shirts, attached by buttons, hooks, and ribbons, embroidered with roses and other floral designs. The vacant ice blue of their eyes watches you from the distant ridges of the Tatras, while from thin pink lips veiled in gentle smiles, they pelt you with shrill words of a passionate song you don't understand.

Your nirvana subsides when you feel a tingle in your crotch and realize you have misplaced your porno magazine somewhere within this landscape of cliffs and white flowers. You are digging through the grass, fumbling for anywhere you can find a decent two-page spread to get off on. You can't believe you would be this dumb to lose such an item all alone in the wilderness.

There is a rumble in the distance. The spring day rips with the crack of thunder, and lightning strikes you not once or twice but many times, the coy sun now rolling away behind the incoming gray, having had enough of its flirtatious game. A rain falls, a thick rain, wetter than most. You slick your drenched hair back like a greaser and look up into the sky to realize that this is no rain. A great bird, a double-headed eagle, is pissing down on you in a torrent. You open your mouth in awe only for it to be filled with this bird's urine, choking you back to reality, as lightning continues to strike your body again and again.

You are on 19th Street and Kedzie but not inside the house. You are crumpled in the back alleyway surrounded by broken glass and a loose dangling power line. A stray cat is inspecting you, sniffing curiously, and scampers off as you fully wake. Your whole body is bruised in pain. You roll your legs over only to discover your crotch is soaked with piss. Your eyes are not opening all the way, and when you move to touch your brow, you wince. The skin is cut and swollen thick, coated with dried blood.

It is morning. You are trying to remember what happened at the party the previous night. All you can recall is staring at a beautiful woman as a dog attempted to hump your leg. You attempt to prop yourself up, but the pain is too great. Your legs are too damaged. You shout for help.

A man walks up to you through the alleyway. "Thank God, man," you manage to groan, "Help me please! I need to go to the fuckin' hospital!" Possibly the man doesn't speak English. He stares at you, emotionless, with bright brown eyes and gelled black hair shaved on the sides and long in the back, an outdated mullet. He kneels down to you, and you reach out to take his hand. Instead of an embrace to pull you to your feet, this man reaches into the pocket of your wet pants, pulls out your wallet and walks away.

You pass out again, and you wake up in the hospital. You are being wheeled around on a bed, your whole-body throbbing in pain. "Help me ..." you mutter. "Help me ..." You fall in and out of sleep, waking up to see bright lights above you, men and women in scrubs staring down at you, changing IV's, taking vitals, jotting notes. The only thing consistent between your deep sleep and blurry moments in the gurney are the dully repetitive beeps of machines pulsing in the room around you, in and out of your vacant dreams. Briefly, you think you see your mother over you, shaking her head.

An unmeasurable amount of time has passed, and you are discharged from the hospital with many interesting new scars and a cast upon your left leg. You wiggle your tongue on your gums and touch a finger to your mouth to face the reality that one of your front teeth is missing. At home you can't stop looking in the mirror, examining your appearance, attempting to come to terms with the new landscape of your body.

You can only gather that you did something seriously wrong in that trap house. Something to warrant a severe beating such as this. But you know that isn't you. You are a good guy. People like you. Deep down you know you are all about respect. Drama free. There had to be some sort of misunderstanding along the way.

* * *

"You are not invincible," your mother tells you in the doorway. She has brought you your pain medication, prescribed after the incident.

"No shit, Mom."

"Hey! Dupek ... listen, I know you have hate in you. But you can't run from the past by being just as reckless. Do you think that this is what your papa would have wanted?"

"Don't talk about him to me!" You raise your voice. "What could he have wanted for me that he could have found at the end of a rope?"

"Well, what about what *I* want for you?" she sighs. But it is too late. You have slammed the door to your room and are swallowing pills, which soon knock you out into the deepest of sleeps.

* * *

Four crackheads are meeting up by the benches on the platform of the Jackson Blue Line CTA stop under the streets of downtown, looking to score. Three men and one woman. They merge by the trash cans, rummaging hands in pockets, then fingers through the thick of their scalps. Their faces are brown and weathered, scarred, eyes faded with disenchantment, lips blistered, skin ashen. They anxiously scratch their necks and cheeks and fumble with the keypad of their "burner" phones with prepaid minutes in the age of smart devices. Their boisterous voices carry through the tunnel, announcing their authenticity to the tourists and transplants around them, waiting on their commutes, as if to say, *This is Chicago. We own this bitch.*

"Hey, Dolla Bill!" one man calls out to another, moving in for a complicated handshake and stopping Bill right in his tracks. "What's good, baby?"

"What up, Stop Sign?" Dolla Bill says to him.

"Just another day! That's all! We out here on the streets of Chicago!" The woman in the group is sitting on the wooden bench, blasting house music from a portable speaker, fiddling with the large hoops in her ears. "Hell yeah!" Stop Sign continues. "Hey, Gypsy! Ey! Ey, Gypsy!"

"What?" Gypsy coughs with a throaty croak. Her faded beauty is mysterious to you. A long scar down her right cheek and rough sunken skin masks the young woman she once was. "I'm tryin' a get hold of Dante! You got his new number?"

"I got it, baby," the third man says, walking up to the rest of the group.

"Old School!" Gypsy shouts. "Where you been?"

"Been livin', baby. Been livin'," Old School says. "Here let me call Dante."

"Ey, Stop Sign! Got a dollar?" Dolla Bill asks.

"Fuck outta heah!" Stop Sign says, passing Bill off with a wave of both hands, "Hey, Gypsy, you holdin'?"

"I'm tryin' a get a hold of Dante!"

"We out here! Chicago, baby! Chicago *made* house music! This my jam!" Old School shouts through a wide-open mouth of yellow broken teeth. He dials Dante's phone number while dancing in place to Gypsy's music. He lets the phone ring with the speaker on, so the whole tunnel can hear. It rings twice, then a robotic white male's voice says, "The number you are trying to dial is no longer in service. Please hang up and try again."

"Mothafucka didn't pay his goddamn phone bill!" Gypsy sneers. She spits on the ground and stands up to pace and think.

Another friend of this group comes down the escalator from the street-level entrance. By the time he is passing you, Stop Sign is already in his face to greet him, stopping him dead in his tracks. "What's up, muhfucka?" Stop Sign asks. The newcomer laughs and turns his head to you. He reads your face and knows you are an outsider to the situation but is good hearted enough to fill you in.

"Oh shit, it's Stop Sign!" He laughs again and says to you, "See they call him Stop Sign cause he'll stop right in front of you and check you! Talk your ear off ... That over there be Gypsy. Girl is as slick as a gypsy. She'll steal the watch right off your wrist if you not careful. Maybe stab you too. And that boy Dolla Bill. He always comin' round axin' everybody for a dollar. And him, that's Old School."

"Why do they call him that?" you ask out of politeness.

"Old School? Well, he just old school!" The man belts out another hearty laugh deep from the gut.

"Well, who are you?"

"Me? I'm Tony."

"I thought you'd have a funny name," you say.

"Well, what's your name?"

"Spider."

"Ha! What the fuck kinda name is Spider, buster? That's what I'ma call you! Buster! Cause you must be bustin' my balls!"

"Hey, Dante ain't pickin' up!" Gypsy yells over to Tony. The whole time you have been talking to this man, the group has been hollering and arguing over each other in the background.

"Ey, I got a connect! Let me call him!"

"Call him!"

"Yeah, whaddaya waitin' for?"

Tony pulls out his cell phone and calls a number while his counterparts shuffle around and bop their heads to Gypsy's house tracks. When the other line answers, Tony discretely makes plans, says "Uh huh" a bunch of times and hangs up just as the train to Forest Park starts to pull into the station with a whistle, a rumble of wheels, and a set of headlights flooding the off-yellow dimness of the faded tungsten bulbs above the stained cement platform.

"Come on, let's go!" The group cheers and shouts, dancing onto the packed train car, celebrating the process of being able to score. The train's bells ring out, and the doors slide closed, and you are left with the remnants of an absurd slice of life. A lifestyle so absurd that it is staggeringly real. All you can think about as you wait to take the train northwest to the River's Casino in Rosemont is that you never, ever, not in a million years, want to turn out like them.

* * *

You have ingested a cocktail of Xanax and Miller Lite and are taking the CTA Orange Line northeast toward downtown in a blurry stupor, heading to your job in the meat department of the Treasure Island Foods on the Gold Coast. Your black apron is already slung around your neck and tied around your back under your unzipped flight jacket. You wear your company baseball cap flipped backwards and snapped loose upon your head. Your eyes are sinking into your cheeks. You continuously wipe at your face, red and drenched in sweat.

At the 35th and Archer stop in McKinley Park, a woman boards the car and sits in the row of seats across from you. You pay no mind to her at first until you realize how long she has been staring at you, trying to make sense of who you are and what you're about. She says something, but you miss it under the rattling of the train car. She repeats herself, and you realize she has said your name. Your birth name.

"Spider? I guess Spider's what they call you now," she clarifies.

"All my friends call me Spider."

"Do you remember me?"

"No ..."

"We went to high school together. Victoria."

"I don't know ..."

"We were science lab partners. We had a couple classes together."

"Vic ... toria ..." You say staring off through her. Your skin feels tight around your bloodshot eyes. You can barely focus on the confused face staring back at you.

"Are you okay? You're really sweating."

"I'm great ... I'm really great, dude. I'm a butcher now. I'm going to work to chop the meat." You give a crooked smile and make a chopping motion with your hand as a meat cleaver onto your other hand, the piece of beef.

"That's great, Spider," she says, but her eyes are swollen with concern, her lips curved and dangling open. You choke some puke up from your gut and catch it in your mouth with bulging cheeks before it can spill out onto your work apron. Victoria watches you swallow the bile back down with a deep gulping choke, saying nothing.

"Well, it was great catching up with you, dude," she finally tells you. "I gotta go ..." You flip a passive wave to her before slinking back into your seat and rolling your head onto your left shoulder, closing your eyes. When you open them again, it is to the chiming bells of your transfer stop downtown. You fall forward from your seat and catch your hands on the aisle pole, careening your head around in search of your bearings with an abrasive slack to your jaw. Before you exit the train, you notice Victoria never left the car. She is staring at the glowing screen of her phone by the doors on the other end. You wave to her again, but she pretends not to notice. Outside of the train car, you are met with the blinding light of the midafternoon and the muddled sounds of the city as you shield your brow and mutter *bitch* under your breath.

* * *

Your buddy Jose, from the neighborhood, has a cousin who does cheap tattoos out of his apartment in Little Village on a block right near the border of the Latin Kings and Two Six territory.

"Bring 50 bucks and a case of beer, and we good," Jose said. Now you are standing on the corner of 26th Street and Whipple, staring at the red archway over the street reading "Bienvenidos a La Villita" that connects into a white marble pillar draped in a Mexican flag on either side of the road.

You stop in an Aguas Calientes restaurant and get some tacos. You get al pastor. Jose gets cow brains. At the corner store afterwards, he grabs a case of Tecate and a packet of spiced crickets. People are staring at you. You feel exotic here. It is not every day a hulking goon of a white boy walks into this area.

Around a corner you find the apartment number, hit the bell, and are buzzed in to walk up a decrepit staircase enclosed by chipped drywall tagged with magnum Sharpies and paint pens, upper corners towards the ceiling draped with cobwebs consuming hordes of house flies. Norteño music blasts from inside the apartment, so you knock on the door extra hard. "Chingada madre…" a man groans. You didn't notice the constant buzzing sound of the tattoo machine until it ceased.

A man opens the door. His face is weathered and serious with a heavy brow ridge. He wears a white wife-beater and is covered in black tattoos from his skull to his throat down to his arms and hands. "Quien es este güero?" he asks.

"That's my buddy, güey!" Jose stands up for you.

"Hey, man, I'm Spider." You hold out your hand. Jose's cousin looks down at your hand and holds out his elbow to bump yours with. His hands are covered in black latex gloves. "What's your name?" you ask.

"You can call me Sancho," he tells you.

"Good to finally meet you, Sancho."

"He's fucking with you!" Jose laughs. "His name's Roberto."

"Come on in, man," Roberto says. "Throw that beer in the fridge. What you getting done today?"

"Well, I wanted to get a black widow on my neck."

"Man, what's up with you guys and spiders? You guys butt buddies, güey?" He shows you the stencil of the giant spiderweb tattoo that Jose is getting over his bare skull. You also notice the hyena cackles of three young gangbangers hanging in the kitchen, drinking tequila straight from a bottle, and cracking bottles of Modelo, peeling back the gold foil of the necks and tossing it on the ground while they wait for their friend to finish getting tattooed.

They eye you up and down in silence, an act of intimidation you have grown accustomed to over the years. You say hello to them, but they still say nothing. On their foreheads or necks or cheeks are tattoos of Latin King crowns, tear drops, or initials in Old English font. You throw the Tecate in the fridge, and only until you make your way back into the living room do they start joking and cackling again. The Norteño switches to cumbia, and one of the more drunken boys starts dancing with the tequila bottle in a gentle swagger, pretending it is a beautiful woman, kissing it on the lips before chugging a swig and wiping his mouth.

Conocí una señora en la ciudad de Monterrey...

When the other guy gets out of the chair and bandaged up, Jose reveals his head is buzzed and razored completely to the scalp. Roberto applies the stencil and begins to tattoo. You watch the black ink lines eat away at the purple stencil covering his dome, spreading little beads of blood.

When Jose's tattoo is finished up, his skull is swelled up like a mushroom. He winces as Roberto wipes off the pooling smears of ink and blood with a squeeze from his green soap bottle and a thick sweep of a bunched-up paper towel.

"Check it out," Roberto says. Jose walks to the mirror on the wall and gives himself a look up and down, turning his head to see as much as he can of the tattoo. "It's badass, no? Here, I'll take a photo with my phone so you can see. I, uh, don't got a bandage that can fit your skull though, so you might wanna go across the street to find something."

"Órale, güey ... It's tight, bro. It's fuckin' tight." Jose turns his head down for Roberto to snap a photo.

Some time has passed, and Roberto has drawn a simple traditional style tattoo of a black widow and stenciled it on to the side of your neck with transfer paper.

You stare at the purple transfer lines in the mirror with a pursed-lip nod of approval, one hand scratching the stubble below your chin in admiration. You feel as if this tattoo is symbolic, the start of many big changes in your life. You will be legit now. Your identity will soon be solidified in ink. There is no turning back. You are Spider for life. Wind is finally blowing in the sails of your fate.

"You ready?" Roberto asks. You nod, furrowing your brow in readiness to embrace the oncoming pain. The first line still comes as a surprise, and you draw your head back in reaction to the buzzing shock burning wet on your skin and rattling your neck all the way to the bones in your throat and tissue within your ears. "Can't do that shit, Spider, if you don't want me to fuck it up! Jose, I thought you said your boy can hang?"

"I can't force a guy to have a spine, güey!"

"Ah, fuck outta here ..."

"Come on, let's go. Stay still this time!" The Latin Kings in the kitchen laugh at you as the buzzing starts up again, and you draw your brows tighter, forcing yourself to endure the discomfort.

Midway through your tattoo, after Roberto finishes the lines and goes on to the shading, the gangbanger who danced with the tequila bottle is passed out on a couch, snoring in front of the speakers that disgorge the bouncing horns and accordion of banda music, which reminds you of your father's old polka tracks. The other boys are plotting in the kitchen, pointing at their friend. Through narrowed eyes and a turned head, you watch their plan unfold.

Each gangster unzips his pants, whips out his penis, and brings it above his sleeping friend's face. Jose is already bursting out laughing. Roberto's hand slips a bit in distraction. You hope it won't be noticeable in the finished product. He stops his machine and turns to the three boys who are now pissing all over their friend who quickly wakes up, flailing, spitting, and sputtering his lips, grimacing. "A la verrrrga!" he yells, and everyone laughs. Even you briefly.

"Get that shit outta here!" Roberto is waving them away with his rotary machine in his hand. The boy who was pissed on is throwing punches and grappling with his friends. Jose has his hands to his face, shaking his head in hysterics. "Get the fuck outta here, bro! I got a fuckin' customer! Head ass ..."

The agitators howl, "Woo! Woo!" and make a break down the stairs, laughing, followed by their sopping friend.

"Just gotta add some red on the back, and you got yourself a black widow, homie," Roberto tells you.

"Dammmnnn, boy, looks sick!" Jose is smiling.

"You think so?"

"Oh, hell yeah, Spider." The boost of pride from this compliment gets you through the pain of the rest of the tattoo.

You and Jose both pay Roberto and drink a Tecate, then head out to find a bandage for Jose's head. "Let's go to the Discount Mall in the lot across the street. They got everything," he tells you. You say your goodbyes and step outside to the early evening.

The Little Village Discount Mall is not like most malls you have been in. It is one large single level building consisting of a labyrinth of independent vendor stalls diverging into different paths and aisles around the premises. In the first stalls are charro outfits and sombreros for mariachis as well as cheap used guitars, violins, cellos, and accordions. Other stalls have soccer track suits of the Mexican national team and graphic tees. Some sell serapes, jewelry, hand-woven clothes, roses in globes, prayer candles, worry dolls, and other trinkets. Others sell comales and brown clay pots to cook beans in, handpainted with blue and yellow designs. As you pass this stall, a woman is speaking in vibrant Spanish to another woman who is about to purchase a pot.

"What is she saying?" you ask.

"She says, 'If you use this pot, you will cook the beans so right that your husband will never beat you again.'"

"Really?"

"Something like that ..."

You turn a corner, and an old man is vending gigantic tropical birds, colored bright blue, green, red, and yellow, with sharp curved beaks that click and whistle with flicking tongues. Beady eyes animate and rotate mechanically, while gripped talons slide and adjust on wooden poles, making sense of you, the newcomer, from behind the tight wire cages that barely allow their massive wingspans to breathe. In an aquarium tank next to the birds is a school of orange and white fish, half the bodies swimming, and the other half floating upside-down towards the top. Past that are box cages of ferrets and chinchillas.

"Ey, Spider!" Jose calls. "I got it!" You turn to your friend who is opening a package of adult diapers, ripping a single pouch open to tape over the swelling abrasion on his shaved head. "This should heal'er up good." He smiles. You can't help but smirk. Together you walk out of the Discount Mall into the dusk streets of La Villita, you with a bandage pad heavily Scotch-taped to the side of your neck and Jose with a puffy diaper strapped over the tattoo on his skull. Somehow you have never felt tougher.

* * *

You have been fired from your job in the meat department, which is why you are currently getting out of bed and pouring yourself a bowl of cereal at 5 p.m. on a Saturday evening. Your mother must be out getting groceries or sitting in the park where she likes to look for four-leaf clovers. You stare at her ceramic ornament of a crucified Jesus nailed onto the wall above the kitchen table and remember the day on the Orange Line meeting your old classmate.

"Victoria ..." you say to yourself. "Yeah, Victoria. We had classes together. She was a nice girl."

* * *

You are standing under the lighthouse of Barnegat Light off the edge of the inlet, watching the Swiss cheese moon dip into the purple ocean horizon. The light of Old Barney sweeps in circles, screeching and whistling in perpetuity. The last of the sleepless sea birds flap their wings in silhouettes across the glow in the sky. You are at peace with life, with God, with fate. But now you are hearing thick slaps echo out over the wall of ocean soundscapes. The slaps fade in like dials pressed slowly forward on a mixing board in a studio filled with smoke, dim red bulbs, and plates of drugs next to rolled-up dollar bills on wooden tables adorned with shaded lamps.

You swing open the doors of the lighthouse and begin ascending an infinite amount of curving stairs, only briefly pausing in your struggle to peep out the oval windows cracked open to let in the salt of the breeze. Your body is trudging now as if through a deep muck, moving in slow motion no matter how hard you push forward. The slapping is so loud now it beats the drums of your ears in a tribal rhythm. In what seems like a lifetime of movement through cuts of stop-motion film, you are finally at the top banister of the lighthouse, the beacon surging through your clothes and skin as a life-force. You gaze across the sleeping island, then to the fishing ships floating across the golden moon in celestial tides.

The slaps draw back to heavy quarter notes. You pull out a long telescope from your jeans pocket and extend its parts as far as you can reach, pinching your left eye and putting your right pupil up to the glass. Through a black circular vignette, you are witnessing your father sitting on the edge of a shooting star, legs dangling off, with you sprawled over his lap, your jeans pulled down and plump buttocks round and open faced to the heavens and outer space. With his left hand he holds your head. With his right he draws back his wrist and spanks your ass with a clapping smack heard light-years away.

You gawk at the sight of yourself, mouth and eyes open wide. For a moment the shooting star and your father are lost behind the churn of Old Barney's light. When he reappears, your father looks more like a Betty Boop character, drawn in black, gray, and white. His eyes are sarcastic ovals with deep slits. His head bobs eerily to a rickety cascade of a piano melody. His mouth is long and smiling, full of overbearing square teeth that mock you.

"Bydudu bydudu bydudu, buh, buh, bye, Boo Boo Bear!" he stutters and shouts, his eyes bulging in a comical wink that coincides with the chiming of a small bell, like the opening of a cash register. He spanks your pale ass one last time, and the shooting star rips him soaring across the arc of the moon and away through the galaxy into some far dimension. You drop the telescope and rub your eyes in disbelief with two four-fingered white-gloved fists as the trumpets and "oom-pah" drums play out the end of the episode and the red curtained screen closes in on your face.

* * *

You are walking into the Kedzie Orange Line Station when you hear a frantic voice sobbing around the corner. "Fuck this shit, bro! Homie dead, bro. Blasted in the back. Pussy-ass got 'em in the back! I seen that shit! Bullet went straight through his skull, bro. Homie's brains were on the street. Fuck this shit, bro. Dead ass. Shit's fucked, bro. I can't do this, bro. Shit's fucked. Shit's fucked. Bro, I can't do this shit no more. Help me, man. Please! Oh God! You gotta help me. Do somethin'. All my homies dead, bro ..." Through the window you can see a tall tattooed man in a fitted White Sox cap crying recklessly on the phone. His body is convulsing as he sniffles and wipes his eyes, head shaking. "I can't do this no more. Bro, I stepped in his brains, runnin'! That was my boy! Jesus, it hurts too bad. A course I ran, bro! It fuckin' hurts, dude ... C'mon ..." His sobbing trails off as you make your way up the escalator to the platform.

You remember the day you went over to a friend's house in middle school whose father worked nights at the Steel and Wire Factory. As he slept snoring on the couch through a walrus mustache, hands rested on the paunch of his hairy gut and legs stretched onto the coffee table in front of a droning TV, your buddy showed you the secret cabinet where his father kept his hand gun. You held that Ruger American Pistol in your palm, feeling the strength and courage of an army flow through you. Finger on the trigger, you pointed it to your pal, who hurriedly ducked and slipped onto the floor, howling, then to a mirror where you watched yourself wield the weapon at your own image.

You felt like a thug, a gangster. A street hooligan type hoodlum. Until your buddy's crying woke his sleeping father and the image of an angry shirtless working man rose behind you in the looking glass, lips cocked in a sneer, mustached like a broom, fueled with the mechanical rage of the factory line.

Your mother beat you upside the head until your ears rang in a panicked daze. You were sent to bed early with no dinner and sat awake through the night in the shadows of your room, facing the dawning reality that you had no clue who you were or where you were going. You were not a thug in the least. Just a confused kid.

Now the bells chime for the train headed toward Midway, and you think you can still hear the gangster crying below you, the fear of death ringing behind his eyes. But the ringing is just the doors closing. And you look down and out the window to see if you can catch a glimpse of the man on the phone, but you can't, and you are left wondering about the seemingly random events and choices forced on all of us in a life that delivers us by the hand to our fates.

* * *

You are standing on a short cliffside patched with grass and rocks on the edge of a vast lake riddled with small islands stretching out into the pink horizon. Thousands of people balance on the edge of the cliffside around you, holding onto roots, rocks, or the branches of trees to hang off as best they can to be closer to the water without falling in. Their faces are anxious, chanting in anticipation, singing off-key pub ballads like English football hooligans to hype themselves up for what comes next. *You'll never waaaalk aloooone!* Clouds are drawing in on the sunset. The energy amongst the crowd rises, and you know whatever is going to happen is going to happen soon.

"Bully Boy!" a voice shouts cutting through the chanting. "Bully Boy! Come here!" You turn and see a young man with a black eye and spiky blond hair waving and calling to you.

"No one has ever called me that," you tell the man as you approach. "My name's Spider."

"Bully Boy!" he repeats. "Come on! It's time! Get ready, buddy! Let's goooooo!"

The crowd roars as a great horn blows a deep resounding tone across the vast cavity of the lake below the cliffside. People are throwing themselves headlong off the edge into the water with a religious courage, catapulting off rocks, swinging off tree branches like apes, tumbling down the dirt of the cliff face, cannonball diving, jack knives, reverse somersaults, the more crazed participants doing belly flops onto the now turbulent water. A few just breast-stroke straight off the cliff out into the sky and fly away until they are nothing but specks.

The man with the spiked blond hair runs to jump, but his his right foot trips on a root toward the edge of the cliff face, causing him to flail down the side, snapping his leg. He bounces off rocks and dirt and crumples into the water with a weak scream. You decide you do not want to dive into the water, but it is too late. The crowd behind you is pushing forward like a bulldozer, and all you can do is embrace the fall.

As soon as you splash into the lake, you have become a child again, wearing a bright orange life vest. You begin dog paddling as best you can across the stretch of the water. Everyone has become a child. Some with arm floaties, or on rafts, or with inner tubes. The less fortunate ones have no lifeline and are forced to swim or sink into the depths, while the rest paddle past their drowning bodies.

By the time you reach the first island, many of the kids around you have given up and made camp there. This is the end of the line for them. They are too frozen with fear to move on. They watch the rest of the children pass, waving gently with waterlogged chubby fingers, trying to remember the words their mothers taught them to say to departing friends. "Bye-bye! Bye-bye!"

Gray clouds spit rain down upon you as you dog paddle past the island. A Band-Aid floats up from the water into your face. Its white pad is stained red with someone else's blood. You spit in disgust and push it out of your way, but more used Band-Aids and bandages pop out of the water now, and the crowd of swimming children has become so dense and concentrated at this point in the lake that none of you can escape this issue. The children next to you now have thick leeches sucking on their bare skin.

You roll over in your life vest and face back towards the previous island to see that the waving babies are now gray old men with thick beards down to their knees, holding great wooden staffs carved from tree branches. Their faces are forlorn, exhausted with the knowledge of suffering and endurance of labor during their time on this earth, though still they wave gently. "Bye-bye! Bye-bye!"

The children behind you are pushing forward, while you are still facing back, and you are smothered under their dog-paddling strokes to get forward in the great race of life, buried beneath the waters of the lake filled with weeds, leeches, fish, and an unfathomable number of bloody Band-Aids floating in the murky brown. You gasp desperately for any chance at a breath of fresh air.

* * *

"Yeah, I ride with the Boozefighters. Shit, we're older than the Hell's Angels! But I ain't no one-percenter. We do pay our respects though. Don't get me wrong, the Boozefighters were there during the Hollister Riots."

"Hollister Riots?" you ask. You are drunkenly standing outside a dive bar near Chinatown where a long row of motorcycles has lined up on the street to party. The man you are talking to is barrel chested in a tight black shirt for a local moto-works worn under a leather vest patched with the Boozefighters MC insignia. He wears a black flat cap pulled down over his brow ridge. His eyes are dark and serious. On his left cheek is a line-drawing tattoo of an anchor. His throat is covered in one giant piece that expands across the sides of his neck. To the left of him stands his woman, a burly girl with pin-up-style curled blond hair and a pouting face thick with gaudy makeup. She smacks on a piece of gum with an open mouth and stares through you, saying nothing.

"Yeah, the Hollister Riots," the man continues, "four-thousand bikers showed up to Hollister, California, for the annual Gypsy Tour after World War II. They took over the whole town, drinking, fighting, fucking, and sleeping in the streets. They laid waste to everything around them. It was the first time bikers were seen as a threat to the American way of life. The police couldn't stop them. The AMA said the trouble was caused by the one percent deviant that tarnishes the reputation of motorcyclists. The other 99 percent are decent, law-abiding citizens. My group of Boozefighters, we're old—for us, our list of priorities are family, job, and club, in that order. But for one-percenters it's club, then family, and job. Look, I'm in my thirties. It's too late for me to be a gangbanger on a motorcycle. Don't get me wrong, I am a bad guy!" He laughs at his own joke, and you crack a brief smile. "Seriously, I do bad, bad things."

You run your hands over the seat of his chopper, failing to notice the tension rising in the Boozefighter's eyes. "This is a nice bike!" you say. You are drunken warm with whiskey and coke. You feel easy and free. Your lips are curved in a natural smile. "Hey, man! I ought to get myself one these babies! This shit's pretty cool!" You laugh and turn to high-five him, bumping the stand of his chopper out with your foot and knocking the bike onto the ground with an abrasive clank and crash that pierces the ears and hearts of all the motorcyclists around you on the block.

"Dude ..." your acquaintance says to you, almost exasperated that he has to kick your ass. You look down to his chopper, then back up to him in time to get uppercut into the gutter where you stay down and cover yourself until your punishment is over.

* * *

It is September, and you and your buddy Michał are headed downtown to catch the Brown Line North to Laschet's Inn for Oktoberfest food and imported German draught beer. A night at the Podlasie Club off Milwaukee Ave. lies ahead. Gone are your days of hard drugs together, but you can still enjoy a pint or three in each other's company.

Your train pulls into Clark and Lake, and you make the transfer up the stairs and over the tracks to the other platform. On your way back down the stairs, a man passes you, looking into your eyes. "Crack and dope. I got crack and dope."

"Nah, man. We're good," you say, laughing. You notice Michał looking back at the man behind you, and you can tell he has the itch.

The schedule on the digital screen reads the train isn't coming for 15 minutes. Since you didn't wear jackets, you decide to wait between the two glass doorways heading into the building connected to the station.

"Look at that guy," you say to Michał. "That's the plug." You point to an old black man standing by the escalator to the building. Every so often a group of haggard men and women approach him, quickly interact, mess around with a lighter and go on their way, cackling and shoving through the glass doorway onto the tracks. Their stench is always rotten, their faces scarred and dirty, their eyes faded. Their lack of care for their wellbeing intimidates you, but you maintain a poker face. They are wild cards. People who care so little that they can do anything and it wouldn't be out of the ordinary. "Look, he just sterilized a needle for that woman with his lighter! What happened to this place?"

"He's gotta be making a killing up here." Michał laughs. "This is a central point for all the junkies and crackheads in the city."

The woman who just scored walks through the glass doors, pushing her hair back behind the large hoops in her ears. Her beauty has faded into abrasions and sores. "Ey! Ey! Wait up!" she calls to her friends in a croaking voice.

"Gypsy?" you say to her instinctively. It was years ago when you first saw her. She looks to you, almost more surprised than you are that you know her name.

"Who the fuck are you?" she asks, slamming the door open to approach a man who is doubled over in euphoria on the train platform. Somehow he manages to stand, his face down by his crotch, hands hanging past his knees, neither alive nor dead, just high. All the addicts are congregating around him now. Some are dancing. Some mumble along to current rap songs. Others smoke out of pipes openly while their friends get in each other's faces and yell incoherently. The commuting business people of downtown do their best to avoid eye contact, keeping headphones on and faces down into their newspapers and smart phones. You turn to say more to Michał, but he is inside the connecting building attempting to buy drugs, relapsing back to his old ways.

"Dupa, come on! What are you doing, bud?"

"Ey, just for tonight, man, like old times. It will be fun." He tries to smile at you.

"I got that factory job now, man! It's union. I get drug tested. I can't fuck that up for this!"

The Brown Line towards Kimbal pulls into the station, and the bell rings for the doors to open.

"Just one night ain't gonna hurt! What? They're gonna drug test you tomorrow?"

"No, but ..."

"Next week then? Come on, live a little, dude. You've been dead inside since you started over there." The second bell of the train rings, and a pre-recorded voice says *Doors closing*. You shake your head.

"Do *you,* man ..."

"What?" Michał stammers, passing his money to the dealer below his waist.

"I said just do *you,* man. I'm outta here." You push through the glass doors and past the circus of junkies and barely make it onto the train before the doors fully shut. The Brown Line car rumbles and heads out over the Chicago River, the skyscrapers of downtown shimmering in the sunset. It pulls through River North, Gold Coast, Lincoln Park, and up to the North Side, and now you feel stupid for having even come this far. You sit at the bar drinking a brown Dunkel in a tall glass next to a plate of schnitzel, wondering if you'll ever see your friend again.

* * *

At 24th and Oakley, a random strip of classic Chicago Italian restaurants is planted in the heart of Pilsen. Little nonnas are being escorted out of a café by their grandsons across the block. You and your buddy Feliks stop into one at random because a Ford Model A is parked out front, refurbished into working condition. The paint job shines like it's 1927.

"Ignotz's, huh? Wanna check it out?" Feliks asks.

"Says you enter through the alley."

"You call that an alley?"

You and your pal walk through the narrow space between the two buildings to a back door that opens to a room bustling with life unseen from the view of the street.

Oil paintings of the Old World decorate the walls next to framed maps of Venice and Sicily. Blackhawks pennants break up the monotony of Italian heritage, along with modern televisions playing world hockey games between Russia and Canada. Frank Sinatra croons over the PA system. Servers push small tables together to fit large families with faces of Dick Tracy cartoon characters, the oldest surviving nonnas at the head of each grouping. By the wooden bar, a man with gray slicked-back hair, a sunken face, and a gray mustache, leans his bushy forearms onto the counter to pick up the ringing telephone.

"Hello, Ignotz's! Oh, hello, Father! Yes, this Sunday. Of course, I always got a seat for you. I put you right next to the sisters. Hey, how about those Bears? Uh huh. Alright, see you after mass."

The tables are full, so you and Feliks sit at the bar. When the man gets off the phone, he comes over with menus and introduces himself as the owner, offering you each a shot of Amaro on such a fine day. You've never had Amaro. The bitter herbal liqueur wets your tongue and sloshes between your cheeks. Before you fully swallow, you know you'll be ordering another.

Now, you and Feliks are sitting at the bar in the early evening. The lunch rush is over, and you pick at what's left of your pasta and sip neat Amaro not saying much to each other in the lull before the dinner crowd.

A woman sits at the bar a few stools down. An older woman. An Italian woman. Drunk on digestifs, you can't help but stare. Her hair is sprayed with volume. Short gold rings hang from her ears. Her lips are an ochre that complements her olive skin. She keeps looking back to you, stirring the straw of her drink with well-manicured fingers. You don't know if you are making her uncomfortable.

"Why don't you talk to her?" Feliks asks.

"What?"

"The lady over there. She's beautiful. She's looking right at you."

"Well, don't make it obvious," you say, seeing the woman down the counter smile and sip her drink.

"Well, what's wrong with you, Spider?"

"What do you mean *what's wrong* with me?"

"How come you never bring no girls around? All this time I've known you, I've never seen you get close with girls. I mean, I know we aren't prized pigs, but all of our friends have at least had girlfriends before."

"Man, just shut up."

"What are you a gay or somethin'?"

"You think I'm gay? Come on, man, you've seen me fight two guys at once before!"

"Tough guys can be gay too, Spider. I'm not judging. I'm just sayin'."

"Sounds like you're judging."

"I'm not! Jesus Christ!"

"Then what?"

"I'm just sayin' ..."

"Look," you tell Feliks, leaning in, "you want me to be honest?"

"That's what I'm sayin'!"

"If you really want me to be honest. I never been with a girl."

"Ha! I knew it."

"Hey! Come on! Listen!" You talk close to Feliks's face to be discrete. "It's not cause I'm gay or nothin'. It's ... well ... fuck, man ... it's just that some ... well ... some real bad shit happened to me when I was young. It kind of turned me off from sex for a while if you know what I'm sayin'."

"What? Did the priest get you? Ha!" Feliks laughs. "A young guy like you not wanting to fuck ..."

"Fuck off! I'm serious, man! I never told anyone that before. Not even my parents."

"So, it was the priest?"

"No, it wasn't the priest! Jesus, just shut up. It *did* happen though, and it scarred me. Just be a good friend for a fuckin' second."

"Look, man, I'm sorry," Feliks says, lowering his voice. "I just thought you were chicken-shit or something. I didn't know."

"I'm chicken-shit?" you say, shooting Feliks a fed-up look.

"No, I just thought that for a second before you explained everything is what I'm saying …"

"I'm chicken-shit, huh?" you say, getting up and shoving in your bar stool. Feliks drunkenly laughs and throws his hands in the air.

"Ey, Spider! Where are you going?"

"Well, if it means so goddamn much to you, I'm gonna say hi to her!"

"Well, what about what you were saying!"

"Just shut up for two seconds, all right?"

You walk over to the woman at the end of the bar, hardly noticing her smiling at the owner who is walking back into the kitchen, trying not to burst out laughing. The phone rings on the counter, and he is forced to come pick it up.

"Hello? Yes, Deacon Giovanni! I've got you down for 2 p.m. Sunday right after mass. No, no, nothing's funny! It's something else. Say, hey, I think the Sox are going to have a winning team next year!"

You sit down at the bar next to the woman. She finishes her drink with the straw through the side of her lips while she stares at you, waiting for you to speak. Her eyes are a deep brown that reflects the bar lights. You stare at the streaks of burnt orange around her pupils and lose track of all your words.

"Well?" she says to you.

"Sorry about my friend."

"Your friend?"

"Feliks over there." You point over to your buddy who dismisses you with a pout and a wave and pretends to watch the hockey on TV.

"Oh, him? I'm not interested in him."

"No?"

"I'm interested in *you*." She smiles. You laugh nervously, fully understanding this woman is far more experienced and confident than you in the games of sex and love. A lifetime of bulldog fearlessness causing trouble on the streets couldn't summon the courage for you to keep looking her in the eyes. It's your childhood, you tell yourself. It's not your fault, but you can't go like this forever. It gets worse the longer in life you wait. You just have to power through.

"What's your name?" you manage to ask.

"Aulina."

"I'm Spider."

"You're so spooky, Spider," Aulina laughs. "What came first the nickname or the tattoo?"

"The nickname, the nickname."

"I bet you get asked that a lot."

"A little bit."

"You drinking?"

"Well, I already drank. Ha, I don't know if I need anymore."

"Then you want to get out of here?"

"Where to?"

"For a drive?"

"I don't have a car." You smile, cheeks flushing red.

"Mine's out front. I'll drive."

You pay your tab and say goodbye to Feliks who insists on staying at Ignotz's to catch the end of the game. Aulina takes you by the hand and walks you out through the alley, squeezing against the walls of the buildings as bodies brush by, heading in for the dinner rush.

"So where's your car?" you say when you get out front.

"Right here." Aulina smiles, nodding to the Ford Model A parked next to you.

You get in together, and Aulina starts the car with only a little trouble. It pouts and spits and cools to a rumbling purr. She pulls it out of her parking spot and heads north on Oakley towards 23rd Street, a natural at shifting gears, while the bystanders in the neighborhood gawk and wave as you pass by.

This is the first genuine feeling of class you have felt since your father rented your family a house on the Jersey Shore when you were a kid. But this feeling is different. It is between you and a beautiful woman in a vintage machine not readily available to anyone. And the kicker to you is that this woman could have chosen anyone to ride with her, and out of everyone in the neighborhood, Aulina chose you.

"My family has owned property here since the '40s," Aulina explains. She is wearing large sunglasses as she drives and lets go of the steering wheel to light herself a cigarette. She turns the car onto 18th Street, passing Angel's Tire Shop and its assortment of used bicycles lined out on the road next to stacks and stacks of rubber tires and displays of weathered antique furniture. A rooster cries and struts down the sidewalk, bobbing its head and crimson tail feathers in a march of arrogance, though it jumps in fright when Aulina honks the goofy horn of the Model A and laughs hysterically at her own joke.

"You're cute," you tell her.

"I know," she says. Your chest is bursting with emotion, a mix of excitement and anxiousness.

Neither of you say anything for a moment as you pass the green of Harrison Park where Pilsen locals have set up blankets for picnics, hung hammocks between trees, organized baseball, soccer, and volleyball games, as others play frisbee or fly kites with friends, and dogs chase each other freely, only pausing to urinate. Young punk rockers with spiky hair sit on the metal bleachers, drinking 40-ounce malt liquor and commiserating. On the tennis courts, tennis is not played, rather young Mexican women have used the smooth surface to roller skate figure eights and smoke marijuana to the soundtrack of boom boxes playing banda music on the basketball courts next door.

Aulina's Model A passes taquerías and tamalerías, Sabores de Michoacán, panaderías and lavanderías. She stops to let a mother and child cross to the paletero ringing his bell by the underpass to the Pink Line train where the old bums drink out of brown bags and spit and scowl at passersby. Two have scuffled into the street, ripping each other's shirts off and cursing with Mexican slang that is hard for you to decipher. Aulina pulls through, and pigeons scatter. You both smile at their fearful coos. The Pink Line train swoops in with a heavy rattle, and when the racket is over, you look to Aulina and want to say something, whatever you can to keep the moment going.

"Thank you," you say.

She laughs. "Thank you for what?"

"For this!" You gesture your hands around. "This is the happiest I've been in a long while."

"Well, you are welcome, Mr. Spider!"

Aulina turns South on Ashland and West on Cermak, making her way back to the hidden pocket of Italy inside of Little Mexico. She pulls the car up Oakley and parks not in front of Ignotz's but in front of an apartment building.

"Where are we?" you ask.

"This is my place," she says. "Would you like to come up?"

* * *

In Aulina's apartment she fixes you both Fernet and Cokes. You sit on her leather couch and analyze the mix of Old-World Italian heirlooms, new age bohemian furniture, and local art on the walls. Together you make small talk. You are just glad to be in a woman's company. Not because it proves your doubting friends wrong but because for once doing so is starting to make sense.

"Look," Aulina says. "I heard what your friend was saying to you in the restaurant. Busting your balls and everything."

"You heard that?"

"Of course, I did. Hah, he was practically forcing me to listen."

"I'm sorry."

"No, you don't understand." Aulina corrects you with a hand to your thigh before reaching to light herself another cigarette. "I want you to know that I'm not judging you. It is okay to have gone through what you did and be scarred from it. It is okay to wait. To experience things later."

"It is?"

"Of course it is! You do still want to wait, do you?"

"Me? Uh, I don't know. Maybe not anymore. Do you?"

"I'm at your speed, Spider." Aulina smiles. Your chest is rushing with water, but you force yourself to do the unthinkable. Now or never, you convince yourself and draw in your lips for a kiss. Aulina is caught off guard and smiles before drawing back into you, putting her cigarette out hastily on the wood of the coffee table with her free hand.

Together you and Aulina rock in an embrace on the couch, exploring each other's clothes and bodies with your fingertips, slowly kissing with closed eyes and heavy breaths. Aulina unbuttons her blouse and unclips her bra to expose her tan breasts, and you reciprocate by taking off your shirt, knowing you are far too deep into this endeavor to fall back into your fears. Before the evening is over you have opened a Pandora's box, a brand-new vice cast upon your life. But where your other vices are self-destructive and heavy handed, this vice is warm.

It is rhythmic. It is filled with the passion of synchronized breaths and gyrations. It is a thornless rose, beating like a heart. And it feels dangerously close to love in a world that you've built on violence, apathy, drugs, and hate.

***

You are walking toward the train from Aulina's house. You have seen her numerous times now and feel confident, happier, less inclined to get into trouble. You whistle and hum to yourself while you make your way down the block, hands in pockets, with an extra bounce in the rhythm of your strides. But on the next corner over, you pause, seeing a group of brown circular lumps on the ground under one of the trees lining the sidewalk.

Something is rustling in the leaves. You jog forward to see a crow chasing a large squirrel around the trunk and gnarled boughs of the tree. On the concrete are the convulsing bodies of the squirrel's babies, dropped to the ground like balls of dough in the heat of the mother's flight. The baby squirrels breathe slow and heavy. Some have open eyes that glisten like marbles. Below a few of their stomachs are small pools of dark red blood. The mother continues to be chased by the bird. The rustling of feathers and thrust of bodies through the leaves sound out with sharp caws and fearful squealing chirps.

Another baby falls from the tree. You wince at the thud. The babe cries at your feet, breathing in and out in desperation. You pick it up into your palm, saddened by its size. Besides an initial squeal, the squirrel does not struggle. Soon your hand is smeared in red. You wrap the baby up in the fabric of your shirt and take it with you toward your apartment. The least you can do is save this one.

Everyone on your train ride wonders what you are holding in your shirt. You can tell by their stares, the jerks of their heads whenever it lets out a pitiful squeak. You dare not show them. And you don't care to boast. When the bell for your stop rings, you jog out the open doors, doing your best to maintain the comfort of the baby animal.

In your apartment, you wash the squirrel off and dry it gently in a towel, then make the baby a proper bed of blankets in an old basket. It lies there, staring up at you, trying to process everything, in shock.

You bring some water and splash it on its mouth. It doesn't react. Not even to lick its lips. You stare down at the baby squirrel like it is your own kin. And it stares back at you, knowing not what you are, good or bad, but that you are something maintaining its lifeline, and you stare at each other for about two hours. The baby finally stops breathing, causing you, earlier at your happiest, to break down and cry like you did when you were a little boy.

* * *

K-Town. You and Aulina are drinking at your place on Karlov and 47th with her friend Allie and her boyfriend, SD Joe. The two brought over some lighting equipment and an air fryer that they had stolen. Maybe you can sell it for them. Or even better, maybe you can buy it from them.

"You have some eccentric friends here, Aulina," you joke in her ear when the guests are in the other room.

"Like you don't?" she says in a serious tone.

They call Joe SD Joe because he is in the SDs, the Satan's Disciples. Joe is mangy like a dog. His beady eyes reveal an empty head. He talks to you about crimes he's committed while you count how many teeth he has left in his mouth.

"I've been shot and stabbed in the head too many times to count," he tells you. It is something he is proud to announce. It's his version of a college degree. You notice that he isn't scared of anything, but maybe he is too crazy to be brave.

Aulina explains how one summer the head gang banger put a hit on Joe. Anyone who could whack him would get a promotion within the gang. Allie proudly tells you that Joe invited the competition and spent most of his time around Pilsen in plain sight, getting attacked by thugs and kicked out of the local bars.

"I'm a dyin' breed." Joe smiles with his remaining teeth. "Last of the white gangbangers in Chicago."

"And you're from Pilsen?" you ask.

"I killed my first guy at eight years old," he continues, sipping an Old Style, "But my whole family were criminals and murderers. Except for my little brothers. That's really why I went so hard with this. To scare 'em. It's too late for me." He shakes his head and looks to the floor. "But I can still change them."

"Aren't you scared to die, dude? You're practically throwing your life away," Aulina says.

"Dying is the only thing guaranteed to us in life. So why be afraid of it?" Joe says this staring off into the chipped paint of the wall. "The first guy I killed was running away from my dad. I took the gun outta his hand and aimed. Bullet went straight up dude's ass and out 'is stomach. It was natural for me. Fuck, I'd kill my own mother if I had to. Fuck that bitch! Don't get me wrong, I bought her a house with my own cash and shit, but I'll never forgive that bitch for my childhood. No way! But that's the way it is. I'm sayin'. I once whacked a guy and stopped by his mother's house to bring her flowers the next day. She was all sobbing and shit. I told her 'This is who we are. We're thugs. Your son was a thug. This is how we die.' I paid for the whole funeral myself. She even invited me to attend. So I did."

Allie begins explaining that SD Joe isn't scared of cops. He beats them up on occasion. He tests them. He talks shit and smacks their guns away, always fighting against their arrest. They had put him and Allie in a holding cell after a random altercation. He told the cop that he would get out of that cell and whoop his ass, and the cops just laughed in his face and told him "Good luck." So Joe ripped down the sprinkler system off the ceiling and flooded the jail with water. They had to take the prisoners out while they fixed the issue. As they did so, Joe clocked the cop in the face and whipped his dick out to piss on him before being subdued.

"The guy's pulled guns on some of my friends. Knives on others," Aulina tells you. "I think it's his demented way of bonding with other men."

She laughs, and you nod and sip your beer. When you pull the bottle from your lips, SD Joe is right up in your face.

"If you ever hurt Aulina," he says to you, "I'm going to murder you."

"Bitch!" Aulina shouts. "What if you hurt Allie? You know what I'm gonna do to you?"

"Man, I punch that bitch in the face!" Joe scoffs at the end of an incoherent shouting match. Allie falls into a bunch of house plants Aulina brought over. She is all wasted and drugged up. "Equal rights, equal fights!" Joe keeps repeating, not paying attention to his girlfriend passed out in the ferns.

Joe switches his focus back to you. "I'm gonna cut off all your fingers and toes and break your legs, so you can never work again." You don't say anything back but stare right into his eyes and sneer. You are trying to show Aulina you are a good guy. You don't want to be a bruiser in front of her. You want to be a gentleman. The world of having a woman around is still new to you, and you want to cherish it, not tarnish it with violence.

"I'll choke Yuppie Joe to death if I see him around Pilsen without a camera!" SD Joe explains. He reaches toward you to demonstrate a lethal choke. Your eye contact is unfaltering. You let him choke you to prove a point. No matter how tough he thinks he is, you will never give a single shit about him.

"See you gotta press your fingers here on the throat to make it a slow and painful death." Joe says, pressing his thumbs into you.

It is 3 a.m. on a Monday, and Aulina plays '80s house music on your turntable. It quakes through the apartment on your stereo system, while Allie and Aulina drunkenly dance around, shouting things that aren't words. Somehow Aulina manages to dance recklessly and still not spill her Fernet and Coke. She is very beautiful to you in this way.

Joe keeps pressing into your neck. You sneer and look into his vacant eyes, unimpressed while suffocating, until he starts to feel stupid and lets you go.

The guy he wants to kill, named Yuppie Joe, is Aulina's abusive ex-boyfriend. It is another reason SD Joe is called SD Joe, to distinguish the two maniacs.

Allie is falling into more things in the background of your droning conversations. Aulina yawns and says she is tired, but SD Joe is forming himself a line of blow with his train card on the kitchen countertop. You look again, and Allie is passed out crapping on the toilet.

"I'm gonna kill yer ass when you least expect it," Joe continues on and on. "Or maybe I'll take you outside and just hurt you real good. All it takes for me is one punch. I'm known for it."

"Maybe I'll lose," you tell him. "I don't care. It's the principle of it." You are beyond sick of the dick-measuring contest and just want to take Aulina and go to bed.

"Then you're a real man," Joe says. "But I'm still gonna hurt you."

"I know."

"I'm gonna murder you."

"Understood." You have not averted your eyes from him. He turns his head away and mutters about the ways he would kill you.

"What's that?" you ask and stare until he walks back into the kitchen.

Joe and Allie leave after three goodbyes and head up and down your front stairs and back into your apartment two times to piss.

SD Joe has a rickety metal wagon painted red that he left out in your hallway. It looks straight out of a Fourth of July Norman Rockwell painting, except Joe carries all his stolen gear in it. Allie has passed out in the ferns again, and Joe picks her up, lugs her down the stairs like a caveman, then throws her passed out into the red wagon and wheels her limp body away down Karlov like it's a fucking parade, holding one of Aulina's cheap bottles of white wine up to his scraggly mouth to take long swigs and maintain his inebriation.

You slam the door behind them. Back in your bedroom, Aulina is vomiting Fernet into a trash can. She does this until she has exhausted herself enough to fall asleep on your mattress placed on the ground without a bed frame. You were hoping to have sex but decide to sit on the couch and watch television while Aulina snores like a bear. In the middle of the night, you hear a gunshot in the street and a squeal of tires. You flip the channels and pray to God that someone has finally killed SD Joe for good.

* * *

Aulina likes to go to the karaoke bars on the North Side. You have just finished singing "Ace of Spades" by Motorhead in a dingy establishment on Milwaukee Avenue in Avondale for an audience consisting half of karaoke-night attendees and half of motorcyclists. The bikers cheer and slap you high-fives, happy to hear a dirty, upbeat song. Most of the other performers have been singing ballads or sad-sap tunes. Aulina gets up to the microphone and begins singing "Kiss Me Deadly" by Lita Ford.

Aulina is sauced on Fernet and Cokes. You have come to find that she always is. Her voice is raspy and slurred, and her harmonization is shaky. Instead of singing the tune she is more so shouting in some vague form of melody. At first all the male bikers laugh and give a round of applause to the chagrin of their leather-clad girlfriends. But as the song continues to play through, Aulina is having a hard time standing up straight. Fewer words make it into the microphone.

To save her performance, Aulina makes her way to the bar counter with the wireless mic and props her platform heels up on a barstool and then onto the bar itself, staggering across the line of drunks, making her way around bottles and glassware. "Oh, like you could do better!" she shouts at a booing audience member. "Oh, what's up, Axl Rose? What's up, Judas Priest?" she shouts at an unamused biker dressed hat to boots in black leather and a blue bandana around his skull. You have to admit the scene she is making is pretty punk rock.

When it comes time for the chorus, Aulina shouts it. Her platform heels slip on a wet spot on the counter, and she falls tits over ass off the bar, knocking full glasses of beer onto the floor with an abrasive shatter.

"Kiss Me Deadly" is still playing full volume instrumentally in the background, though the groans of the crowd and squeal of the microphone sound over it as you rush to pick Aulina up off the ground, flushed with embarrassment.

"How did you get this drunk?" you ask.

"I pissed myself," she says. "Get me the fuck out of here ..."

"Get her the fuck out of here!" the bartender yells.

"Yeah, get her out of here!" some of the biker's wives and girlfriends shout.

"Fake-ass bikers!" Aulina shouts and laughs to herself before spitting on the ground.

"What the fuck was that?" you ask when she gets outside. "How did you get so fucked up? You on pills or something?"

"I thought you could hang!" Aulina laughs. You had an ideal of this woman when you first met her at Ignotz's and rode in the Model A. That image proved to be a fantasy relatively fast.

"I thought I knew who you were ..." you say. But she is not listening. Aulina is talking shit under her breath, muttering things that don't make sense and laughing to herself about them. One of the female bikers comes out of the bar, and they exchange words. You think things are gonna be heated again. You wave down a Flash Cab and put Aulina in it headed home.

"You're not coming?" she asks. You stare at her for a second.

"No."

"Fine. Fuck you then."

"See ya, Aulina."

"See ya never."

You wave down the next cab and head home to call it a night.

* * *

You are riding home in the cab on the highway, staring at the distant silhouetted buildings of Downtown. They're scattered with yellow lights, and a halo glows into the starless sky above while Top 40 pop music plays on the car radio. You look at the cabbie's license, laminated and displayed facing towards you from the back passenger seat. You want to say something. Anything to get your mind off Aulina and the stinging feeling that you will be alone again in the world of love.

"Djordje is your name?" you ask. He grunts and nods. "Where are you from?"

"I am Serbian," Djordje tells you in a thick accent.

"No shit. You like it out here?"

"It is good. The winter, however, is no very good."

"You have family out here?"

"Just a few cousins," he says after yawning. "I stay with them in Waukegan."

"So why'd you leave Serbia? If you don't mind my asking."

"There's more opportunity here. I miss it, but I can make more money, send money home to Balkans. My cousins drive trucks inter-state. Me, I drive cab. Only problem is city very expensive. So I live in Waukegan and commute to work here. This takes me all over the city North Side, South Side, West Side. I've been in some very terri-ble neighborhoods. Honestly, I don't really like it. Having strangers behind me in here. I don't know who I can trust."

"Well, where I live used to be kind of shitty, but it's getting better now. It's still cheap though, that's why I like it," you tell him. He says nothing back. "Do you like living in Waukegan?"

"It's okay," Djordje says, "but the only issue is there are too many Mexicans and Blacks. Do you know what I am saying? Always causing trouble in neighborhood."

You do not know what Djordje is saying, and you say nothing back to this. You have grown up around Mexican and Black people. You imagine in Serbia Djordje has grown up only around white Serbians. It was this way in the neighborhoods of Stara Polonia, but not for a long time. You feel guilty for not speaking up, for not explaining to him, but for the rest of the ride you say nothing to Djordje, and when you step out of the car to your house, you realize your silence was just the same as agreement.

* * *

You are on Jackson and State Street downtown in mid-December. Snow is falling from the white sky. Red-bowed ribbons and spiraling green garlands stretch the sidewalks and lamp posts intertwined with white Christmas lights. Below the skyscrapers, fold-out signs read, *Caution: Watch for falling ice.*

By the Red Line entrances, speakers play holiday classics that echo through the cold over the honking of cars, murmur of voices, and rumble of trains encircling the elevated tracks of the Loop. Salvation Army volunteers ring handbells up and down in a lazy rhythm, while across the block, the State Street Preacher wears a deep wool coat and a scarf as he recites scriptures into a cheap microphone, letting the passersby know they will be going to Hell while the flurries tickle his bushy eyebrows.

"scuse me, brother, you got a dollar to spare for new shoes?" an old man asks you, frost clinging to his haggard beard. Behind him, a line of homeless men sit together on the concrete, rubbing hands and shivering. You look down to this man's shoes, and they are nothing but shreds of brown canvas taped on top of a frozen foot beneath a torn sock.

"Just a dollar," the man says again. "Please I need new shoes."

"Fuck it, man, I'll just buy you a whole new pair of shoes," you tell him with no emotion left in your face.

"Really?"

"Yeah. Fuck it. C'mon. Let's go." You start walking towards the DSW store down the street, and this man and one of his friends follow you. You don't have much to say to one another, but you can tell the man is excited. You are not sure what his friend is doing coming along.

At the entrance to DSW, a security guard stops your group. "Oh, not you again," he tells the two homeless men. "I can't let you in. I'm sorry. I can't, guys."

"They're with me. I'm getting shoes," you tell him. He looks to you and then over to them, and they nod. He apologizes and lets you by, though you note his eyes following you around the store.

The two homeless men are feeling up all the shoes, enjoying the warmth of the indoors. "Any of 'em?" Your guy smiles at you.

"Yeah, sure." You nod. You look, and the man's friend is off somewhere else in the store.

He picks a pair of 70-dollar sneakers. You check out and hand the man his shoes. You get him a new pack of socks too, and he changes into both things immediately, thanking you graciously. Before you exit, an alarm sounds off by the doorway, and the security guard is chasing the friend of the homeless man out into the street. The man holds two boxes of shoes and a packet of socks in his hands, running as fast as he can on his frost-bitten feet until he is tackled.

"Let's go. Let's go!" says the man you bought shoes for.

"What about your friend?"

"He'll be fine. Let's go. Let's get out of here!"

Together you walk out into the decorated streets. The snowfall is heavier. The lights of the city are warmer, and the temperature has dropped. "Come with me," says the man.

"Where?" you ask.

"Just come on."

It is your turn to follow this man. Still, you have nothing much to say to each other. Not that much all in common. He takes you to a side street by the METRA Station where massive steel grates are letting out bellows of heat onto a sidewalk packed with people of the streets. "Ey!" your acquaintance shouts to them. "Ey! Look at this!"

He shows off his new shoes. Other men admire the quality and style. He hands some of his socks out to the group. Aside from the ones you bought him he has stolen two other packets. You couldn't care less. You are just entertained enough to continue watching what is going on. The men are cracking booze and bottom-shelf 7/11 wine. They smoke cigarettes, and some have weed. They offer you some, and you step up to the heaters, feeling the warmth of a lion's roar breathing upon your rosy cheeks.

You are one with the crowd of men now, bundled up against their bodies. Their beards scratch your face. You can see their abrasions and the sores of their hands from the cold. You take a swig of E&J Brandy from a short bottle and feel it fill your belly with warmth. The ground is as white as the sky, and the falling snow fills the void between the two. The whole city has become a vapid grayscale. It is as bleak as a tundra, but your heart is warm with brandy and brotherhood, stuffed between jackets of vagrant men you just met, drinking, smoking, pissing, and cajoling for money, howling with laughter at the simplest or most absurd jokes you might have ever heard, but at least in your case, you have decided you feel happy, and lucky to be a tourist to this way of life, and for this to be a pick-me-up, although for the men of the street this is a harrowing reality.

Bells ring out from the train station, and they are no different than the bells of the winter solstice. The season of open hearts has arrived. You praise the complexities of man, brotherhood, booze, the turning and the dying of the earth. A death for rebirth.

"Merry Christmas," you say to the man you bought shoes for, heartily slapping him on the back. He looks you up and down, drunk off convenience store wine, burps, and says to you, "Got a light, buddy?"

You burst out laughing. A deep, gay laugh, out of the ordinary for the likes of you. You hold your lighter out to him and produce a flame. He takes the whole thing from your hands and walks away into the crowd.

NA ZAWSZE

Diego makes his way through the crowd of the bar with a half-empty fifth of Bushmills in his hand and his entourage in tow. You are working the door at The Sweet Misery where Diego DJ's monthly sets, as he is a popular local musician who brings in a slew of regulars to watch him spin industrial and old hardcore punk deep-cut seven inches. Despite his drunkenness, you had to let him in. He is friends with the owner, and he pushed by you before you could even say hello.

Diego stumbles to the nearest open barstool and slams his fifth of Bushmills on the counter. He wears sandals, exposing the stubs of his four missing toes, removed from gangrene due to heroin use in the heyday of his touring. His thick brown dreadlocks drape over his back and fall in front of his pierced eyebrows, nose bridge, and ear cartilage, and his tribal tattooed cheeks.

"Diego!" Al Tucker, your boss, calls out to him, pouring a lager off the brass taps. "You can't bring your own booze in here! C'mon, buddy. This is my bar!"

Diego grunts some profanities, and his entourage of crusty metalheads and drugged-up punk rockers snickers behind him, never ceasing to be entertained by his self-destructive antics.

"C'mon, Diego! I have Bushmills here. Get that bottle out of here," Al says.

Diego looks your boss in the eyes and turns his bottle of Bushmills straight up in the air and to his lips, chugging the second half of his fifth of Irish whiskey down his throat like it is water on a summer's day. He slams the empty bottle down on the bar and releases a deep burp, inciting more laughter from his entourage. He looks to Al and slaps the bar twice with his hands. "Double Bushmills neat!" Diego growls before his head slams down into the counter.

"C'mon! C'mon! Get him out of here!" Al is yelling to Diego's friends.

You stand there at the door, perplexed and hesitant to help. You are fed up with being a door guy. You were hired to be a bartender, not to carry out drunk junkies and break up fights between reckless idiots. Instead, Al decided when he wasn't bartending, the shifts would be filled by voluptuous punk rock girls with dyed hair, piercings, and tattoos. Your place would be at the door, a goon to greet the alcoholics, to politely warn them, "Do not fuck up. I will be the first and last person that you see in this establishment."

Diego's entourage has lifted his limp body into the air. They carry him over their heads like he is crowd surfing. It looks like a bizarre sort of funeral procession as they walk him toward the door. He regains consciousness as they exit and grumbles curses and flips middle fingers towards Al.

"I never liked you anyway!" is one of the few coherent sentences that can be made out between the profanities. The bar crowd jeers at him. Someone throws an empty can in his direction. Still aloft, Diego brushes by you and spits at your feet. You shove his friends in the back, knocking them out the door and into the street where they stumble and drop Diego onto the concrete. He grunts and rolls around in the gutter.

"Don't let that guy in here anymore, Spider," Al says to you from behind. You turn around, and he hands you a bar towel and a spray bottle of sanitizer. "Wipe that area up, would you?" You take the rag and disinfectant and make your way to Diego's seat where the barstool has been knocked over, to clean up his mess of spit, germs, and Bushmills Irish Whiskey that never made it past his lips.

* * *

It is your first day at work, where you have been hired to help Al reopen The Sweet Misery, which used to be his dive bar, Tucker's, dubbed, Fucker's by the locals of Lincoln Park, before it was shut down by the city for health code and liquor license issues. You are in the side gangway with a hose, power-washing the thick discolored mold off the side of the building. Around 70 beer kegs, half barrels, and smaller pony sleeves are lined up down the gangway, leftover from the last time the bar was open. Some are barrel aged and vintage beers meant to last a few years, others are domestics such as Hamms and Budweiser, which surely have skunked by now.

You finish power washing the walls and move on to wash the mold and dirt off the aging beer kegs. Your shoes are soaked with excess spray that streams down the concrete towards the metal-grated drains by the rat-infested dumpsters. After hosing the kegs down, you take white bar rags and wipe the barrels dry until the rags are a deep mucky brown.

You take the 70 kegs and, one by one, roll and carry them inside the bar to the back stairwell, which leads up the three floors of the establishment. You stack each keg in alphabetical order up the wooden flights of stairs, straining your lower back and shoulders as you do. By the end of the process, your right knee stings in sharp pain when it bends.

* * *

It is the next day, and your job is to power-wash the keg cooler, which is also thick with mold. You spray the walls and ceiling for a good 15 minutes before going at it with more white bar rags and mold-removal spray, scrubbing with your hands to erase the stains in the wood. When this job is done, you leave the keg-cooler door open to air dry and broom the excess water into the nearest drain before mopping up the last of it.

In the downstairs, Al has a backbar of 1,000 bottles of liquor held up by wooden panels, bending deep with weight and age in front of a dirty glass mirror for the drunken patrons to watch themselves in. One by one, you dust each bottle and stock it on the shelf, rattling off the name, alcohol percentage and price per ounce to Al, who jots the information onto a spreadsheet on his computer to take inventory and create the new menu.

You scrub the whole keg cooler with another round of mold remover and let it dry for another day with the door open. In this time, you dust, stock, and inventory all the upstairs bar's bottles of booze and wipe the mold and dirt off the old bottles of beer leftover from Tucker's, which will be served to customers at the new Sweet Misery. You power-wash and scrub the standing and drop beer coolers before stocking the two-year-old beer bottles between the metal grates and flipping the switch on to see if the air still flows properly.

* * *

The next order of business is to repaint the keg cooler. You use a whole tub of white paint, a roller, and three different sized brushes dipped into a tray to paint the walls and ceilings twice over the course of two days. Large spiders crawl up your arm and through your hair as you paint crevices no one will ever see with a smooth coat of shining white.

* * *

Al has handed you a metal tool that looks something like a spatula with a rubber handle. "There's about 20 years' worth of gum stuck on the underside of this bar," he tells you. "I need you to scrape it off and throw it in the garbage. And when you're done, I have all the bar furniture in a U-Haul in the loading zone. Bar stools, tables, couches, the pool table and pinball machine. We need to get all that off the truck, dust it, scrape the gum off, and then bring them inside after mopping all the floors." He folds up his laptop and heads up to his office to punch more numbers, leaving you with a gum-stripping spatula in your hand. You shake your head and sigh.

* * *

The last order of business is to take deliveries of bar products, straws, napkins, jiggers, towels, glassware, pour spouts, and the like. In the time between deliveries, you scrub the toilets on all three floors and dust any bottles Al thinks weren't dusted properly the first time. Then you carry large boxes up to the third-floor storage room where you stack them by product in a shaky leaning tower of cardboard.

When you come back down from the last delivery, Al has brought you a slice of pepperoni pizza. "Cheers, Spider," he says, handing you a bottle of Miller Lite, aged about two years, which you hand-scrubbed the mold off of just a few days before. You shrug and pop the cap to drink it. You can't tell if it tastes skunked or not.

"Spider, I wanted to talk to you," Al says through a mouthful of pizza. "First off, I want to thank you for all your hard work helping me reopen this place. Second, I know I hired you for the bartending shift, but I got some girls coming in that have some actual experience behind the bar. They've been doing this for years now. They can rock it out, you know what I'm saying? So, for now, how about let's start you off at the door to gain some bar experience and once you've got acquainted with it for a while we will talk about a promotion?"

You don't know what to say. It is not what you expected to be doing, but you need the money. You were hoping for a more glamorous position, one where you could talk to pretty girls and make big tips for popping caps off beers. You are not scared to be a bouncer, just let down. You shake Al's hand and reluctantly agree.

* * *

"Oh shit, Fucker's is back open!" laughs a man at the door on opening day.

"Hey, bud, can I see your ID?" you ask him, holding up your pointer finger and thumb in the shape of a driver's license.

"Really?" the man scoffs. "I've been coming to Tucker's since before you were born! I'm old enough to be your dad!"

You nod and say nothing, trying to swallow your pride. You have heard this line regurgitated almost word for word three times today already. The man brushes by you, and you resist the urge to punch him back into the 1980s where he belongs. You need the job. You need the money. It is too early in the game to be acting like a fool.

* * *

Rats die weekly in the dirt crawlspace below The Sweet Misery. The stench of their decaying bodies floats into the first-floor barroom where death lingers only to be masked by the smell of smoke curling in the dim red lights from Al striking matches and candles throughout the course of each night.

It is your job to retrieve the bodies of the rats. And though it sickens you to do so, the position proves to be lucrative over time.

Al offers fifty dollars a rat corpse. You are the only employee crazy or desperate enough to take him up on this offer. Other staff members are ex-suburbanite art-school dropouts with parental back-up plans or have double-income households with no children and prime bartending shifts. You have bills to pay. You crawl below the bar to score.

You take Al's keychain and unlock the groaning metal doors, orange with rust, to enter the space below the bar, hands gloved with black latex and your t-shirt pulled up over your mouth and nose. You hold a white trash bag and a small black flashlight in front of you as you crawl on your hands and knees through the reek of mold and rot of death between the base of the establishment and the damp cool dirt, teaming with squirming purple worms, militant ants, brown spiders, and centipedes.

Something rustles through your hair, and you swipe a tiny creature off your forehead and onto your arm and flash your light to see a brown cockroach scattering off into the void around you. You brush a cobweb off a panel and make your way further into the space where the decay smells heavier and pan your flashlight back and forth upon the ground.

The first corpse you find is covered in maggots eating into the dead rat's stomach. Its eyes are already removed. Trying not to throw up, you turn the trash bag inside out, the way a dog owner would do to pick up a piece of poop and grab the surprisingly stiff body with your hand screened by the plastic before flipping the inside back out again, gagging repeatedly.

The second rat corpse is not too far off from the first on the far end of the building toward the property of the Mexican restaurant behind the bar. The stench isn't as bad. The body is fresher. It still has its eyes. They stare blankly at you, reflecting the shine of your flashlight in unholy black beads. You put your flashlight between your teeth, chomping down to hold it still, and palm the rat's body into the open trash bag, before tying it off and twisting the top around a few times so absolutely nothing can come out.

"I only have 75 in cash right now," Al tells you in the barroom. "You know I'm good for it. I'll get you tomorrow." Your clothes and skin are stained with muck. You have thrown the bag of dead rats into the back dumpster where they will be inspected by the very much alive rats that lurk there and will likewise die someday, poisoned in the depths of dirt under the bowing wooden boards of The Sweet Misery, only to be returned to their trash-bin home like fallen soldiers, wrapped in a coffin of white plastic tied off haphazardly with a red drawstring knot.

* * *

The first time you meet Tommy Northside is when you stopped in to The Sweet Misery for a beer on your day off. It's Tommy's first shift as the opening bartender, and he sits nursing a Coors Banquet shift beverage at the stool next to you in the haze of the red lightbulbs, candles, and flashing TV screens.

"Name's Tommy Northside," he tells you, putting out his hand. You look him up and down hesitantly before shaking. "I'm the new morning bartender."

"I take it you're from the North Side, Tommy?" you ask out of boredom.

"Well, that's the funny thing. My family is actually from the South Side. But the North Side's where I made my name. Grandfather was from Englewood back in the day, but I've lived in Rogers Park forever."

"Well, cheers, Tommy. Nice to meet you, man." You clink your pints together and listen to the rock music blasting over the speakers.

"This song reminds me of old G'n'R riffs!" he laughs. "Fuckin' first time I went to a Guns and Roses concert was over in Rosemont when I was like twenty or somethin'. Met this girl with a super boring boyfriend. When he went to buy her a beer, I took her back into a port-a-john and fucked her proper on the toilet seat."

"Jesus Christ, man." You shake your head, unimpressed by the infidelity. You want him to stop talking. You want to be left alone. But over the course of working with Tommy Northside you realize that that is the way a lot of people feel about him. You notice the eye rolls at his stories, the sighs, shrugs, slamming of glassware, the way coworkers talk about him when he isn't in the room, and you see him as not so much of an annoyance but as just another guy trying to make his way in a confusing world. So you start being nicer to him, more compassionate. And before you know it you are going out for beers together, a ragtag duo, without much in common, besides maybe an understanding that neither of you would ever fit in to the confines of respectable society. Friends.

You think about the day you met him now as he drives you in his father's Porsche Cayenne, 130 mph down the highway, zipping between cars and trucks, as you hold on to your door handle for dear life.

"When my dad got promoted at Ruger, first thing he did was buy a Porsche. I only have this car for a couple weeks before I get my old one back from the shop," he tells you. "Better take it easy …" Tommy slows the Porsche down to 30 mph on the expressway. Coming up from behind, cars are forced to brake and swerve out of the lane, honking. He maintains this speed, looks in his rearview mirror, and laughs. "Ah, fuck it. One more time!" Tommy slams his foot down on the gas, and the car revs back to 110.

Smog rests above the dark towers of the Chicago skyline off in the distance as the Porsche passes the graffiti-covered concrete buildings of the abandoned silos on the river by Damen Avenue.

"This is just like Go-Karts," Tommy Northside tells you.

"What?" you laugh nervously.

"I've been racing Go-Karts in Indiana every weekend. I show up with my brother and my dad, and we smoke the pro teams with this little kart we bought and fixed up together. They hate us, man. They hate us! They all have team suits and helmets and legitimate gear. They get to the track a day early and practice for the race. Me and my family, we show up the morning of with beers in hand, I'm high as a kite, and in our ramshackle kart, we smoke them every time. They hate us, Spider! It's beautiful! Thinking of driving out to Manchester, New Hampshire, to ride with my cousin next month in a race out there too!"

"No shit …"

"You know, all my life I've been a loser, Spider. All my life, I've been nothing. Been bullied. Been shat on. Been working my fingers to the bone. But this … man, I finally feel like a winner at something! Whoops!" Tommy laughs as he careens the Porsche out of the middle lane just in time to not crash into the braking van in front of him. He steers into the left lane, presses further on the gas, and swerves back, honking and laughing. You look at the cars behind you and notice all the empty beer cans and packets of chaw strewn about the backseat.

"Spider, hold my hand," he tells you.

"What? No!"

"C'mon, Spider. I need you to trust me. You trust me, right?"

"Yeah, kinda. Well, I dunno."

"You've got to trust me, Spider. Hold my hand." He grabs your left palm, and you squeeze your fingers around his reluctantly. The needle on the speedometer is at 120 mph. You turn to Tommy Northside, and he is driving with his eyes closed, one hand in yours, the other gripping the steering wheel.

"What the fuck are you doin' dude?"

"I'm living, Spider! Ha! I'm living!"

"Open your eyes!"

"You've got to put your faith in life, Spider!"

"C'mon!" you shout. Tommy Northside opens his eyes and slows the car down to merge into the right lane.

"Spider, you need to realize. We don't live normal lives. We shouldn't live normal lives. Hell, we couldn't if we wanted to! You know why? Because we live life for ourselves! We live for the absurd! We live, Spider! We live! We live! We live!" Tommy blows through a red light on the highway off-ramp and turns onto South Central Avenue down past Midway Airport.

"You're crazy, bud. Hate to break it to you."

"I love it! I love it, Spider."

"Tommy Northside on the South Side! Here, park up here by the curb."

Tommy pulls up past the sidewalk to park in a diagonal spot on the side of the Karolinka Club. An old Polish man in a gray and blue USMC shirt stands smoking a cigarette outside the side entrance to the building, sizing both of you up as you exit the white Porsche SUV and slam the doors, laughing.

* * *

You are dreaming of a hospital, pristinely clean, bleached white with lights. Paint runs down the walls from the ceiling perpetually, like a waterfall. You slip your finger under the cascading paint and watch the white drip off your hand and onto the tile floor as teardrops.

A gurney slides into your ass and knocks you on your back, steering you away down a hall so white the differences between the rooms are undefinable. It begins to make you nauseous. The light is forcing you to blink repeatedly. You hardly notice you have been wheeled into a new room filled with the buzzing sounds of flies over the beeping of monitors. Two doctors in white lab coats have their backs turned to you by the counter.

"Excuse me! Doctors?" you call to them from the gurney.

The buzzing sound stops, and the doctors turn to you, both with the facial features of green horseflies with bulbous red static eyes and drooping, scissor-like mandibles hanging from their jawlines. Their hairlines are entirely human, a fair brown at mid- to shoulder-length. The male has a balding scalp giving way to green skin. The female's light hair swoops above her eyes like a horse's mane. They give a few confused buzzes in your direction before turning to each other and locking their mandible jaws in a disgustingly romantic embrace.

The waterfall walls of white paint now bleed scarlet, and the bleached white lights of the hospital turn into the insidious red glow of The Sweet Misery. The buzzing of the human flies is no longer within the room. It is inside your skull, growing louder, thicker, as they continue to kiss, until your ears are dripping the same claret as the four walls around you, and you scream to relieve the deep pulsing of the sawing inside your brain.

You wake up in your bedroom in total darkness, completely alone. You look out your window to the scattered stars or maybe just airplanes above the gothic city, and you remember the childhood summer in New Jersey, in awe of the galaxy above the foaming ocean in the night, the light churning from Old Barney, turned by the hands of wailing sea ghosts. You have never felt lonelier than you do now in this bedroom, listening to the purring of passing cars and watching the light pollution block out all that is holy in the universe for the sake of the industries of man. You are lost for direction. You wonder where your passion went or if there was anything you were ever truly passionate about before this. You decide the missing piece is a woman. In the morning you buy a second pillow for your bed, and you give your face a clean shave.

* * *

Before the second pillow on your bed is filled with the resting head of a beautiful woman, it is filled with the curled-up body of a sleeping boxer dog, cuddling you through each night. A customer from The Sweet Misery was giving a litter of puppies away, and through your recent bout of loneliness, your eyes lit up at the photos on her phone. You were more than happy to adopt.

You name the puppy Harley. You whisper his name to him and stroke his brown jowls and boney forehead while he snores in a ball on the pillow next to you, finally comfortable enough to sleep in his new home. Harley is an angel. A darling. A reason to continue living. During the day he is a lot to handle, being a puppy after all. You go on long walks around the neighborhood. You frequent dog parks and beaches where Harley frolics and bounds across fields of grass or sand, looking back at you with the innocence of a small child, to know you are watching, to know you are still with him. You throw him balls, frisbees, sticks, and chew toys. No amount of running is enough to tire him of playing.

At night, he gallops around the house or chases his tail in circles, toenails clicking on the linoleum floors. He paws at the door or at the wall where his leash hangs on a set of hooks, begging to be let outside. He eats his food in sloppy gulps and laps up water with the sloshing of his long purple tongue. He sits by your side at the kitchen table, looks at you with those pure puppy eyes before chewing on the scraps you throw him from your dinners.

When you leave him alone, you hear him barking out the window at you while you walk down the street, and you shake your head and feel your heart drop into your gut. When you come home, he has most likely urinated on the floor. He spins in circles of happiness at your presence. He jumps up with his paws on your legs and licks at your face and barks while you pet him and move to wipe up his mess in the living room. You watch him bark at the robins and squirrels in the trees outside your window like it is a television show. You could watch Harley for an eternity and still be satisfied. When you walk him in parks, you let him off the leash to chase the geese and pigeons and watch them scatter with fearful squawks, flapping their wings desperately to fly away from his sprinting body.

When you are feeling low in energy, or health, or happiness, Harley cuddles up to you on the couch or in the bed. He exposes his bare belly for you to pat and stroke. He shakes his head and lets out brief sneezes from his black wet nose before laying his soft chin back down on your lap where his whiskers tickle the skin of your legs. It is a connection you have never felt before. Different from the connection of your father and mother. You received their love. Now Harley receives yours. But Harley has given you something some say is stronger than love. Harley has given you purpose.

* * *

Your lifeline is a bike ride through a city tunnel in the nighttime. You were birthed on a one-way path with a predetermined exit. The lights are dim and flicker, exposing abandoned trash and balloon graffiti tagged with gang signs. LKK 1-9 with a pitchfork in red and black. Pigeons scamper out of your path as potholes sail in your direction, bumping you up and down, while a bug flies into your open, heavily breathing mouth, causing you to spit and choke.

White scat dots the concrete amidst pools of excess rain water that splashes your tennis shoes as you pass through toward the darkness at the end of the underpass.

This is Chicago. This is the land of the ignored. The city of wind in the empty tunnels of dead-end dreams. This is not New York. This is not Los Angeles. This is the jungle of barren nights with scattered lights in apartments where insomniac artists compose unseen masterpieces, while factory stiffs take sips of coffee in the sweating heat of the sunrise in rooms of cracked drywall and sunken ceilings dripping when it rains.

Drip. Drop. Drip. Drop.

The rent never stops, and the sunrise lights your eyes at the end of the underpass. It is this underpass you bike through every morning, on a public bicycle at the height of the endless nights, where drunks guffaw and break glassware, not caring to be polite, reminiscing of times when they were heroes, now losers, in the red of the dim bulbs, crying, cursing, hoping to impress the rest of the degenerates, to redeem some form of pride, like a currency, to make their failures worth living through. Life is like this underpass, this tunnel. You ride it every night. There is no end in sight. But you know how it ends. You speed out into the darkness to whatever may come next.

* * *

A graveyard never forgets. Like amber, it preserves fossils of memories lost in the depths of centuries. Roots of willow trees, like motherly arms, cradle your loved ones and the rotting forgotten in beds of equal plots of dirt.

It is only fitting that as you and Harley visit your father's headstone, an autumn rain weeps into the orange and yellow blaze strewn about the browning field of grass. *Spoczywaj w Pokoju* it reads with his name and date. *Rest in Peace.* You unfurl your black umbrella above your head. This is the hardest time of year. Harley barks at the murder of crows fluttering towards the red-leafed boughs of a maple tree by the rusted iron gates. He sniffs the wet grass and shakes his head with a sneeze, tracking scents.

A graveyard is a novel. A testament to sonder. A headstone is a bookmark. This is where you last left off. You throw scarlet roses on the stage in praise of their performance. The story of your father's life is read before your eyes, which glaze over as you watch the memories like spliced shots of a film. The sun hides behind the curtain of gray clouds. It doesn't know how to approach you when you are sad and bitter. Who will tend to the roses here once you are gone? The short answer: They will wither.

* * *

Your mother has a *serce ze złota*. You have a *serce z lodu*. Your heart of ice matches the dirty white of the shoveled walks packed into a pile in front of your childhood home. Jagged icicles hang crooked off the roof gutters like glass daggers, sharp and crude, dripping water with the passing seconds of the shining sun. An early winter's afternoon.

"Serduszko," she tells you. "Eat! Eat!"

Your mother hands you a warm bowl of Bigos, Hunter's Stew. She pours a tall glass of Kompot and smiles gently with her eyes. You turn your fork through the mesh of sauerkraut, cabbage, and mushroom, to pick at the cut-up sausage and pieces of pork shoulder and funnel them into your mouth, disregarding the heat.

"Eat now," she motions towards you with her ladle. "I cannot cook for you forever. When you find nice Polish girl to make *wnuczka* with and take care of house?"

"C'mon, Mom!" You snort a laugh through a mouthful of food.

"I know my son is no angel, but you must find love while still young and handsome!" She laughs to herself while ladling Bigos into her bowl. You sip the fruity Kompot, feeling the balanced sweetness wet your tongue, thinking about Aulina and the other relationships you have been in that have failed to launch into anything serious.

"I will. I will," you assure your mother. "I just have to meet the right woman."

* * *

You bring Harley to sit at the door of The Sweet Misery with you the night you meet her. She walks through the door with a graceful aura, bright with innocence, or carelessness, or hope, and she returns your dumbfounded smile before directing her attention to your sleepy puppy, flopped, and moping on the floor.

When she touches his forehead, his tail goes off back and forth, and you laugh together. You ask for her ID, and she obliges. You scan her photo to match her face and take note of her name. Helena. A beautiful name. And she is truly a match to it.

Helena sits down and meets with some friends over whiskey cocktails and dark bottles of domestic beers. You look back to check on the bar every so often, and occasionally your and Helena's eyes meet. There is a connection. You can feel it. A line being reeled in by energy. It is not confirmed until later when she excuses herself from her friends to approach you.

"Can you drink?" she asks.

"Huh?"

"I mean, on the job. Can door guys have a drink here?"

"Uh ...I don't know," you say.

"Then maybe a nightcap?"

"A nightcap's fine."

"Then I'll tell the bartender." She smiles. "After your shift you got a shot on me."

You are silent out of nervousness. It is not every day or even every week you are hit on. "Thank you," you say, smiling with a heart that is full of something, quite possibly of wonder or dare it be joy?

The rest of the night you sit at the door, imagining more interactions with this woman, the possible conversations, the various webbing futures leading to love, or refusal, or even platonic sex. You snap out of your fantasies as you notice Helena kneeling down by your feet, scratching Harley's face and jiggling his jowls, laughing at his willingness to comply and his apathy towards his adoration.

"He's such a good boy! I love him." She smiles up to you. She holds out her hand to you. You look down to her and reach out to pull her to her feet, but instead of gripping your palm, she places a folded bar napkin in it and stands up on her own. "I bought you a drink," she says. "So now you owe me a drink. Let's get one sometime."

"Uh, yeah ... sure. I'm down." You nod. Helena walks out the door without another word. "How will I ..." you start to say after her, until you realize the folded napkin contains her name and number written in red ink.

At the end of your shift, you have cleaned the bar and its glassware, married liquor bottles, restocked beer and booze, and put the chairs up to mop. You let Harley out to go to the bathroom, and now he sits curled by the door with his head on his paws. The bartender is counting her tip money and doing her drawer checkout, while a cigarette hangs loose from her lips between sips of a pint of Schlitz in a plastic cup. Helena has bought you a shot of whiskey. Jim Beam. Instead of shooting it, you sip it slow. Like it is more than a well drink. It has turned to a Pappy Van Winkle through the pleasure of appreciation. *Helena,* you think with a feeling of warmth. You hold the napkin in your fingers and reread the numbers to assure yourself the beautiful woman you talked to was real.

* * *

Your first date. Your buddy Feliks has invited you to Club Europe for a Polish dance night. His cousin Przemysław is visiting from Gdańsk, and he is spinning electronic music in a mostly empty room pulsing with clipping bass and synthesizer. About 15 guys are in the venue, drinking at the bar, leaning against the wall, or moseying up one of the five ladies present besides Helena, trying to spit their game.

The bartender's face is slender with protruding cheekbones and pale blue eyes like a ghost. His hairline recedes a bit and is combed to the side. He wears a wedding band on his middle finger as his ring finger is just a nub and has possibly been cut off. He catches you staring at it as he pulls a beer from the tap, and his eyes show that he doesn't like you.

You return to Helena by the DJ booth where Feliks is telling embarrassing stories about you in your youth. He tells the story of why you are called Spider, and she laughs at your expense, at the lengths you would go to prove your toughness. You don't mind her laughter. You think her voice is pretty. You hand her a drink, and she rubs your back and smiles.

"This is an interesting place," she tells you, and you understand that she thinks it to be tacky.

"We can leave anytime you want."

"I don't understand this music," a woman says, approaching Przemysław, who is scratching vinyl turntables over a bumbling electronic beat with samples of a woman moaning. "Hey, man! Hey! Hey, DJ!" she yells to him. Przemysław removes his headphones and stares at her with the wondrous eyes of a foreigner abroad. "Do you have any Pitbull?" the lady asks.

Przemysław looks to you and then to Feliks and then shakes his head, baffled. "Who the fuck is Pitbull?" he yells in a thick Polish accent before returning to his turntables with his headphones to his ear. Helena laughs uncontrollably. For possibly the first time, you are embarrassed of your friends.

"Hey, Feliks, we're gonna get out of here," you tell your old buddy. You take Helena by the hand and head out of the club.

Across the street from Club Europe is a roller rink with a large crowd spilling out into the street. You notice Helena's eyes. "You wanna go?" you ask her.

"Can we?" She smiles.

Seventies disco music and Motown classics play while you and

Helena hold hands awkwardly, skating in a loop in a crowd of dozens. You glide like a bow across the reverberating strings of the treble-heavy songs. "I like this," Helena tells you. "No offense to your friend, but this is better."

"Yeah, you're right. This is better," you say.

"This is funny," Helena says. "Rolling in circles. It's like a metaphor. I've been skating in circles my whole life."

"Looks like everyone here is used to it."

"You're a funny guy, Spider."

"I'm funny? What's funny about me?"

"Just you. Just this. Just everything. It's all funny. It's not a bad thing. I like it." You don't say anything back to her. You watch the movement of her eyes and try to read beyond her words. "I never come down to the South Side," she says. "I didn't know there were parts like this."

"It's my home," you say proudly.

"It's funny," she says again.

At the end of the night, you call her a cab, and she pecks you on the lips before entering the door you have opened for her. You are left in the cold in a cloud of exhaust with a mixture of warmth and deep confusion within your identity. How are you funny? How is this funny? Helena represents an outsider's viewpoint to your obscure way of life. But how can you keep living and believing in who you are when someone you hope to love can break down your life in a single passing word. It may be funny, but this is all that you really know.

* * *

Despite your funniness, Helena sees you again and again. You have dated for a couple of months when you find yourself returning from a trip to Bobak's Deli with her and stop in to your mother's house on a whim. Your mother makes you both zapiekanka with mushrooms and cheese, and you eat it to please her, though you are already full.

"Spider tells me you were born in Poland?" Helena says to her, and your mother begins to recite stories you have never heard before.

"This is true. In Częstochowa, my father worked wallpaper business. When I was off school, he bring me along to work. But then I used to play football in the streets with the neighborhood kids, like a boy. Not American football but real, real football. And the boys treat me like one of them. I broke my leg, and I could no longer help with my father's wallpaper jobs. I came home broken, and he slapped me upon the head! Ha! It's funny to think now, but not so funny then. Such a serious man!"

Helena has her hands on her chin. You can tell she is in love. And your mother loves that someone will listen to the trivial memories of her life in a way her own son never did. She eats it up and continues.

"Every year during Lent, I marched with my church down the main street of town towards Jasne Góra for mass, wearing white and red dress, holding a replica image of the religious idol. The mother Mary, the black Madonna, Queen of Poland, a slash across her face, and baby Christ crowned with jewels. *Our Lady of Częstochowa.* The townspeople would come and pin tithings to the virgin's image for the diocese. Bands played. People danced. We waited for hours at Jasne Góra to crawl on our knees in prayer around the altar. I even saw John Paul speak there as a girl! It was beautiful memory. When we came to America to finally flee the Soviets, I swore one day I would go back. And listen! I did not go back until my father died! I flew to Warszawa then Krakow and took train to Częstochowa where I walk into town and hand a man in a butcher shop the address on a piece of paper. I say 'Where is this? I am looking for my childhood home.' He was holding a chicken by the neck and a big knife, and he says 'I cannot take you, but my daughter will. One moment please' And he brings down the knife on the chicken's neck and removes its head before going off to find his daughter. When the little girl came out and took my hand, I soon realized she was blind. Her father told her where to take me, and she knew the way by heart. The small blind girl led me through the town that had changed with time and showed me the streets of my childhood. Where I played football. Not American kind, yes, but real, real football. Anyway, they say do not revisit golden memories. There is always darkness in returning to the past."

"Darkness?" Helena asks, picking off a piece of bread from her zapiekanka. "What happened?"

"While I was there, I had to visit grave of my sister."

"Sister?" you say, "I didn't know you had a sister."

"Yes, I had sister. But she died young. November 11. Independence

Day. She was taking nap by the window when fireworks went off. The volume of the explosion shocked her to death. She was just a teen. The family was heartbroken. We used to play with the boys in our neighborhood. We were just like boys ourselves, the way we played. One person make circle with their hands. Another must drop knife from up high down through circle of fingers. We were so young and foolish. We thought we would live forever. I got old, but my sister did not. I went back, and it was so hard to look at her grave."

"I'm so sorry," Helena says.

"It's OK. I am tough woman." Your mother smiles at her. "I can tell you tough woman too." Helena laughs at this and nods. "When I went back," your mother continues, "I took a car to Zakopane and walked up into the Tatras. I felt so lost. So lonely. I hiked alone into the mountainside, foraging for mushrooms under the sleeping knight of the mountain, for hours, reliving the old country. In a Carpathian meadow I came across a patch of szarotka."

"Szarotka?" Helena asks.

"Edelweiss. A white mountain flower. The kind men used to climb the paths to pick to give to their true love. I picked a szarotka from the meadow and took with me back to Częstochowa where I place on my sister's headstone. A symbol of her pure heart. Her individuality. Her love. I never knew a heart so pure again until I had this little boy," she says pinching your cheeks, causing you to flinch and Helena to laugh. "But now, boy not so good. He is something of a scoundrel. Maybe you can help him, Helena. I always tell him, 'Mój drogi, you look and dress like such a bad man! But deep down I know you are still my little szarotka. You just need to look like it! You just need to act like it! Be good! For your poor mother!'"

You scoff and excuse yourself to the bathroom. While sitting on the toilet you hear Helena laughing and interacting with your mother.

"Sometimes, I think I did something wrong," she confides in Helena. "Like I led him down the wrong path. I was supposed to be his North Star. But how could something bright turn his heart so dark?"

"He *is* a good man," Helena assures. "Things were just rough for him. After his father died ..."

"It was not just his father's death. There had to be something more ... I cannot help but blame myself."

"But you can't. You were doing the best you could with what you had."

"Promise me, you take care of him, Helena. Promise keep him happy the way I never could."

"I promise you," Helena says. Your heart hurts. You flush the toilet and walk back into the room, and the two act as if they were talking about something else.

* * *

At the end of the year, your apartment's lease is up, and after some discussion, you move in with Helena in Edgewater on the North Side, right off the Red Line, where she has lived for years. Harley enjoys the long halls of her apartment and scampers up and down, nails clicking on the polished wooden floors. Helena becomes more protective of Harley. She takes it upon herself to help take care of him.

"This food you feed him is garbage," she says. "It's like fast food for dogs. You need to get him something better." You are taken back by her sternness but agree and try to do better.

"He needs better toys," she continues. "These toys are all cheap and busted. You need to play with him more. And he needs a Kong to keep him occupied when we leave him alone. Also, I'm scheduling an appointment to get him neutered. We can't have a dog walking around the neighborhood that's not neutered."

"You're gonna chop off his balls?" you ask in a passive form of protest.

"I'm not going to. The doctor is!" She looks to Harley, who cocks his head and whimpers in confusion.

* * *

Thursdays become your date nights. They are swing dancing nights at the Green Mill, a jazz club next to the old Uptown Theatre, owned by Al Capone in his heyday and still decorated in the interior like the art deco of the gilded age.

You and Helena take the Red Line a few stops down to Lawrence and enter under the green and white neon lights into a dim club filled with swinging drums and ripping horns, while bartenders in white collared shirts, slicked hair, and black ties pour Schlitz and shots of Malort for patrons at red vinyl barstools. Cocktail waitresses in tight black dresses carry circular trays to tables at crescent-shaped booths facing the floor where couples spin and dance to the jazz beat, dressed like the dapper youth of a bygone era. You and Helena join. You are not much of a dancer, and neither is she. But it is the energy, the gesture, the rhythm and physical connection that matters. And the eyes Helena give you when you hold her close in your arms.

The saxophones squeal, and the trumpets blare deep into the night and reverberate into your brain long after you have gone home to make love and sleep the sound sleep of naked romantics cradled in each other's arms. At the foot of the bed, Harley lies across your legs, his head placed across your shin, gently snoring. His stomach puffs slowly in and out with the drawing of each deep breath.

* * *

In the night, you have a dream that you are standing in the middle of 18th Street in Pilsen, by the Pink Line, staring off at the excessive scaffolding on the twin bell towers of St. Adalbert's church. A car screams by, driver laying into its horn, and you look back to the street to see a fawn trotting toward you, delicate eyes gleaming with youth, out of place in the heart of the city filled with trash, pigeon shit, and pothole roads. The fawn is beautiful. Just a child. Its movements are that of a ballet. You can almost hear the strings playing behind the clapping of its hooves on the blacktop.

It draws close, and you reach out to touch it. You know it is scared. You know it will not hurt you. You want to help it. You can feel the mutual energy. What it needs is love. But as it slows to greet you and you open your arms for an embrace, a blast, like a firework, sounds out in the street, and the fawn keels over on the ground bleeding, with a sickening cry, the likes of which you have never heard. You kneel down to comfort it, stroking its bloody side. The eyes that gleamed with youth are now glazed over in the shock of pain. Its lips fumble along with its tongue while it whimpers. It is trying to speak to you.

"Spi ... Spi ... Spider ... Spider!" it manages to say.

"I'm here," you reply. "What? What is it? What can I do?"

"Spider," it repeats. "Spider ..." And it drops its head to the ground and fades off into the next life.

* * *

Your friend Marcus always comes into The Sweet Misery with random items he has collected from his job. He works cleaning up violent crime scenes in a hazmat suit in apartments and buildings all around the city. It's a lucrative position in more ways than one. Besides the pay, which you know is good because he drinks the high-end whiskey on the shelves rarely touched by the regulars, Marcus also has the opportunity to take what he wants from the bodies and bedrooms of the murdered, who often live lives so obscure their memory and possessions will soon be forgotten or discarded into the trash.

"Shit, man," he says, "today I got myself an old Rolleiflex 6x6 off a dead guy in Back of the Yards."

"Rolleiflex?" you ask.

"It's one of them old film cameras. Hard to find these days. This guy took a shotgun to the face. Brains on the walls and shit. Bitch to clean up. Camera was clean though. He kept it in a desk drawer in a case. I bet I could get a grand for it if I sold it in the right place. Hell, maybe I'll take some photos on it first. Learn how to use it."

"That's wild, man. I bet you could get some crazy shots of the crime scenes with that."

"Nah, Spider. That's some snuff-film shit. That ain't my vibe. Ha! Hey, but check this out!" Marcus holds up his left hand and displays a golden band on his ring finger. "I took that motherfucker's wedding ring! Looks good, don't it?"

"You're a sick man, Marcus." You laugh with him.

"It's a sick world, Spider. But chicks wanna fuck a dude with a wedding ring. Mine now!"

"Hey, if you ever see a woman's wedding ring, let me know," you joke.

"You serious? Cause if you're serious, I'll find you one eventually."

"I'm only half joking." You shake your head. "I mean, I would marry Helena. I fucking love that girl, man. Like, fuck it. Why not? I've never had it this good before. Why not make it last forever?"

"You've got stars in your eyes, Spider. I'll keep a look out."

"Well, I mean, you don't have to. I can always save up for one. But, shit, yeah, I would marry Helena. I know it hasn't been that long. But it's about the connection."

"That's love." Marcus nods, bumping your fist. You nod in agreement. "That's love," he repeats walking back to the bar to grab another whiskey.

* * *

It is months later, on Labor Day, when you run into Marcus having a drink on your day off at The Sweet Misery. You spent the day eating blintzes and drinking Okocim at the Taste of Polonia in Jefferson Park while polka bands played, children rode carnival rides, politicians pandered on the microphones between musicians, and vendors sold folk art and tacky track suits embroidered with the national flag.

Now you sit at the counter in the red-lit room of black shadows, an early autumn breeze coming through the cracked open windows. Marcus is excited to see you. He cheers your lager beer with his glass of Willet bourbon and pats you on the back. He says he has something for you.

"Got it off a woman up by Howard and Clark. A cheater. Husband killed her in a crime of passion. Sterilized and polished it up for you." He smiles, pulling out a ring bearing a large diamond, which shines eerily in the dismal red lighting of The Sweet Misery.

"No shit ..." you say, taking it from his hand to inspect it. "How much do you want for it?"

"Eh, just give me about free-fiddy." He laughs.

"Three-fifty?"

"Nah, Spider, it's free. It's a gift. Give it to your girl for fuck's sake!"

You clap hands and pull in for an embrace. Marcus pats you on the back. You start to feel sentimental tears swelling in your eyes, and you realize now you are very drunk.

"Thank you, Marcus. Thank you so much, dude ..."

"C'mon, don't go getting all emotional on me, man! Hey, just invite me to the wedding, and we good, all right?"

"Of course, man. Of course." You bump fists, and you decide you will leave for home after finishing your beer. As the lager slowly pours down your throat and drains from the glass, all you can think about is exactly how you are going to propose and if there's any chance it's actually going to work.

* * *

It is a Thursday in mid-October on Lawrence and Broadway in Uptown. The green and white light bulbs of the Green Mill sign shine with the street lamps under the pink and black smeared sky. The night is filled with trumpets, cascading piano, bopping drums with piccolo snares, stand-up bass, male and female vocals calling back and forth in their lyrics. The beer flows from the brass taps like a foaming winter river. The lines never bleed dry. The dancing never stops. Jive. Two-stepping. Women swinging in swirling dresses by the arms of suspendered men with pomade slicking their hair.

By the counter, where Al Capone used to sit, to view the whole room, friends and enemies alike, as to never be jumped because sometimes friends are worse than enemies, an old man sits in suit and fedora, nursing a Schlitz and a whiskey on the rocks, snapping his fingers in time, face filled with pock marks and ashen, wrinkled with age and wisdom of the streets. The bartender rubs a glass with a dirty white rag and nods his head to the jive of the roaring tunes.

You and Helena stumble out the front door, laughing. Having had your fill of dancing and drinking, you kiss a kiss, more passionate than most, and walk north down Broadway past sleeping bums under tattered blankets, newspaper, and cardboard, past the crowd of hip swing dancers, the other bars of the Uptown strip. You stop Helena under the sign of the closed-down historic Uptown Theatre, and you read the marquee's inscription.

"NOT FOR TODAY BUT FOR ALL TIME." There is something profound to you in the death of the theater inscribed with the fighting words of a legacy. "Will you be with me, Helena?" you say. "Not for today ... but for all time?"

You kneel down and pull out the wedding ring, stolen off the body of a murdered woman just a matter of miles up the road, and you present it to your lover. She grasps her face and breaks down and cries before she can give you an answer. "Yeah?" you ask. "Yes?"

"Yes, a million times yes ..." You kiss over and over and rock in a tight embrace in the darkness of the street under a now black and purple galaxy where light pollution has killed off the stars. Nothing matters more now in all of this than the two of you and your embrace. You hail a cab to take you back to Edgewater.

"We're getting married!" Helena tells the cab driver. "We're fucking getting married!" You all laugh together. Behind you, the streets of Uptown have grown empty. The crowd of the Green Mill has dispersed.

The Red Line croaks by on the rattling elevated tracks, and the bells ring out to the bums under wraps in the gutter and in the storefronts and alleyways. The empty Uptown Theatre still stands there proud and reverent, like a monolith. It has defeated death. Like God, it has learned to live forever. And like those who live forever, its face is solemn, battered with age, the face of stories untold, lost in the annals of history, a million voices, a million lives, like the whispers of ghosts between foundation and four walls.

NOT FOR TODAY. BUT FOR ALL TIME.
FOR ALL TIME. NOT FOR TODAY. BUT FOR
ALL
TIME

* * *

"Fuck the wedding, man," Al Tucker tells you as you start your shift at the door of The Sweet Misery a few weeks later. "I mean, the wedding is great. But it's all about the bachelor party. For my bachelor party, me and a bunch of friends rented a hotel suite on the top floor of a place in the heart of Amsterdam's Red Light District. We had enough booze, plates of drugs, and hookers to last us a whole week. The deal was that as long as you were in the common room of the suite you had to be awake and drinking or doing blow. You only didn't get fucked with if you were lying in your actual bed. And in the common room we had hookers 24/7. The game was that as long as someone else paid, you had to fuck the prostitute. We would fuck with each other, pick the biggest girls possible and pay full price for the full experience. These girls were putting the condoms on our dicks only using their mouths. Some Grade-A shit, Spider. But as long as someone paid, you had to fuck them, no matter what they looked like. But, hey, a penis has no eyes, right? By the end of the week, if I had to cum one more time, I'd be spitting dust! Fuckin' Spider, I tell you, I got teeth marks on my cock older than you've been alive, kid. I've fucked more whores than you've had hot meals! Haha! We went 24/7, Spider. For a whole week. By the end of it, I didn't even know if I wanted to get married. Think about it, Spider, you're still kinda young! You've got a whole life ahead of you! You want the same pussy hole for the rest of your days? Once the ring's on your finger, sex is out the window! It's like a switch! They don't wanna give it up no more! I tell you, those nights in the Red Light District—some of the best nights of my life! All I'm saying is enjoy yourself, Spider. Life doesn't get any better than being surrounded by beautiful women. I should know. I don't have that luxury anymore. Ha! Just kidding. But you know what I mean!"

* * *

Your bachelor party is a little bit different than Al Tucker's. Part of the promise you made to Helena is to leave your old ways behind. So you assured her you didn't want to do anything crazy. Nothing fancy either. You would rather sit and reflect. So Helena invites her father to take you out and get to know him better. Together you sit at a bar called Memories in Rogers Park, slugging Old Styles and not saying much of anything.

Helena's father is a broad-shouldered man with a pot belly like a kettle drum. He wears thick olive-green suspenders strapped to wrinkled slacks over a plain white shirt. His hair is fading, but he combs the strands that are left haphazardly to the side. The rest of his hair is in the thick gray of his dust-broom mustache and on his bushy arms, curling out of his faded traditional Americana tattoos of naked women and swooping eagles.

"Can I smoke in here?" he asks the tired bartender. The skin of her throat sags the same as her cheeks and eyes. You can see a life filled with work and the troubles of the old neighborhood in her empty stare. Rogers Park in the '80s and '90s. Before the yuppies. Days of violence and bed-bug-infested boarding houses swim in her pale brown pupils, the stories of the mental patients cast out homeless into the streets to roam when the hospitals closed down, the tent cities by the Lake Shore Drive off ramps, the drug dealers, the prostitutes, the gang members, domestic altercations.

"Sure, why not?" she sighs. "There's nobody else in here …"

Helena's father lights a cigarette, and you watch the smoke float up from his lips, consuming the air around your heads. "Man to man," he says, turning to you, "I just need to know you're gonna treat Helena right." He puffs on his cigarette and blows the smoke at your face, testing you, seeing how his future son-in-law will react to his authority.

"Of course I will. Helena is the best thing that ever happened to me," you say.

"Thank you." He reaches out his bear-paw fist and shakes your hand. "'cause if you don't, then this is gonna be you!" He grunts and pounds his empty Old Style tallboy into a crumpled circle. He sees your face and starts laughing a raspy laugh that soon turns into a wheezing cough. "Hey, it's too quiet in here! Why don't you put some tunes on the jukebox, kid?" Helena's father hands you two dollars and winks to the old bartender, whose lips crack upward so faintly you can hardly tell if it is a smile.

It goes on like this for a while. When your soon to be father-in-law is nice and drunk, he drives you home to Helena. She is up waiting for you and together you go to bed.

When you are sure she is fast asleep, you call Feliks. Marcus. Michał. Tommy. Any old friend that will answer.

Soon you are picked up in Marcus' work van. Your friends take you to Rosemont to gamble and drink and dance on girls. Then strip club to strip club. Backroom private treatment. Cocaine and pills. Runs to the ATM. Bills wrapped into straws. Swerving down the highway. Laughing. Screaming. Puking. Trying on Marcus's hazmat suit and running around blindly tackling each other. Spray washing passing cars with his cleaning supplies. Stopping on the side of the road to piss between dumpsters in the alleys.

Feliks knows an abandoned restaurant in Portage Park that has an all-night private party. In the back entrance, you each pay 15 dollars to a young Russian guy in a tracksuit and thick ushanka hat and enter an old dining room where a skinny blond DJ with a face full of plastic surgery spins wall-shaking techno and shakes her ass in a short skirt.

Men line the walls, drinking out of red solo cups and straight from glass handles of booze. Behind what was once a bar, a man pours Stolichnaya and Jameson from gigantic plastic bottles into cups mixed with juice or soda and sells them to drunk Slavs for 10 dollars a pop. The people are bloated, sallow, haggard. They eye you and your friends like outsiders. You spit down at your feet and try to sneer, to dampen the tension of their stares. The mood of your bachelor party has dropped. The music is sobering. Soon your eyes are droopy, and your faces sink into your chests in the back of the van.

Marcus takes you to your apartment in the gleam of the morning sun. You pick up Dunkin' Donuts, shower, brush your teeth, then bring the food to your sleeping wife to wake her like you were doing her a favor.

* * *

On a cool spring evening at a banquet hall in Bridgeport, you stand in front of family and friends to present Helena her wedding ring, one you have actually saved up to buy this time, and as the crowd applauds and whistles to the signifying kiss of your knot being tied, a tear falls from your eye. A tear of happiness and relief. It is an otherworldly feeling to you, one you now remember witnessing as a child, in a man and woman on the Jersey shoreline, hugging and dancing, and crying at the fact that they made it through, despite your father's anger.

"You don't know what we've been through for this," you tell the crowd. "Thank you. Thank you all for being here. Especially my mother. I love you so much."

A buffet is served, and a DJ plays house and classic dance hits on a square of wooden flooring surrounded by green carpeting, where friends rock each other into the night, young and old, hearts fanned like a fire that will never be quenched. Outside the earth blooms into pastel flower petals and chartreuse leaves. The city bursts alive like a stricken gong. Together with the earth you have defeated death. You have built something that, for better or worse, through daydreams and nightmares, will live bonded forever inside.

* * *

It is a year into your marriage on a rare evening when your wife draws you into the bedroom, eyes like a cat's, reeling you in on a line with a beckoning finger, and you wriggle, gyrate, and pulse together under white sheets, giving the occasional kick to Harley when he tries to hop on the mattress to play, and just as you are about to climax together and you move to pull yourself out of her, Helena moves her hands to your buttocks and holds you in, turning the feeling of pleasure into that of sobering panic.

"Stay there, Spider. Put a baby in me," she moans, writhing on your phallus which is about to release.

"A baby?"

"Put it in me, Spider. Make me a baby," she says again, gripping your buttocks tighter and pushing you further into her. At the last moment, you rip her hands off you and force yourself out. Your climax is brief. Disrupted by surprise, you quickly deflate and slide off the bed.

"What?" Helena asks. "What's wrong?"

"I'm sorry. I can't do it. I just ... I can't do it."

"Is it too soon?"

"I just ... I don't know when it will be time. I wasn't expecting that."

"I'm sorry," she tells you, pouting in shame. "I thought you would want this too."

"I don't know if I want that. Or when I would want that. I'm just not ready," you tell her, throwing on underwear and pulling on your jeans.

"What are you doing?" Helena asks.

"I'm getting dressed. I need a drink."

"You're going out?"

"Just for one. Do you want to come?"

"Why would I want to come?"

"Because you want to be with me?"

"I want to be with you *here*. Don't you want to be with me?"

"I do. But right now, I could use a beer."

"What are you afraid of? Do I disgust you?"

"I don't know. I'm just scared."

"But of what?"

"Of being a father maybe."

"Or of commitment?"

"I married you, didn't I? You know I have father issues!"

"Well, what can I do?" she stammers.

"I just need time. I need time, and I need a beer." You lace your shoes and throw on a track jacket, blow your wife a kiss, and head out the door to the corner bar where you think about the orange sky above your swinging father and the hole it left in your heart.

* * *

"I'm getting all fat and ugly. I used to be handsome. Now I'm just a big fat lumbering Polack," you tell Tommy Northside before sniffing a bump off a key in his SUV.

"Well, there's your problem, Spider. It's all the drugs. The drugs and the drinking. Bad combo. Many a handsome man's face has shriveled like a raisin due to alcohol."

"Mine's blown up like a pumpkin. I look like a bulldog now. So how do you get away with it?"

"Me? Good genes, Spider. Good genes. Except for my hairline." Tommy laughs, "Here give me a bump. No, come on. Hold it up to my nose for me. I'm driving. There's a cop up there, I need my hands on the wheel."

Tommy rolls up to a stop sign past the cop car and pulls through the intersection. Shortly after, the police SUV turns behind your car and follows you down the block with its lights off. You turn right onto Kedzie at a red light when the red and blue flares with a war whoop, and the officer flags you over to the side of the road.

"Shit," Tommy says, rustling through his compartment drawers for his insurance and registration, "Okay, Spider. Let me do the talking." A floodlight snaps on behind Tommy's SUV, disorienting you both. Then a rap on the window with a nightstick. Tommy rolls it down.

"You know your left taillight is out?" the officer says.

"No, sir, I did not. I'll get that fixed right away, sir." Tommy fumbles over his words.

"Any drugs, alcohol, weapons in the car I should know about?"

"No, sir."

"Who's this?"

"That's my friend, Spider. Just taking him home."

"Spider? That's your Christian name?" He laughs, "Where you live, son?"

"Edgewater," you tell him without looking at his eyes.

"Then you're heading in the wrong direction."

"We were just going to turn around." Tommy smiles.

"You boys been drinking?"

"No, sir. Just one or two," Tommy says.

"Yeah, I can smell it on your breath." The officer frowns. "Step out of the car."

"What?" you protest. Tommy waves to calm you down.

"No, it's okay, Spider. It's fair. We're not drunk, so we have nothing to worry about."

"It's bullshit."

"Your friend's right, *Spider*. C'mon, son, just going to do a couple tests."

The officer shines his light in Tommy's face and makes him balance on one leg for 20 seconds, which Tommy does with ease. He then has Tommy walk a straight line, foot in front of foot, one step at a time, still shining the flashlight bright in his face. When that is over, he has him follow his finger, he tests his eyes and ability to follow instructions. From your seat in the car, you can see Tommy doing nothing wrong. The officer pulls out a breathalyzer test, and Tommy refuses to blow.

"Look, if you don't blow, I'm going to have to take you in," the officer tells him.

"Well, I didn't do anything wrong. And I don't feel I should have to blow."

"Then it's all settled," the officer says, pulling out cuffs and throwing Tommy up against the hood of the car while you shout in protest but don't dare to interfere.

You think back to SD Joe, the man who fought cops on the regular, and you feel a shame in the decline of your toughness as you have cozied in to domestic married life. Still, you do nothing, docile, while the cop takes Tommy off to the local precinct and leaves you with his car on Kedzie, as the vehicles and pedestrians pass by under street lights, wondering what you two must have done to warrant the arrest. You watch their necks crane like rubber, and you look back at them with a sneer.

* * *

"I thought this part of your life was over!" Helena wails, handing you the money to bail out your friend.

"It is. It was just this incident! Look, I know he would do the same for me! He's gonna pay us back. He's good for it!"

"It's not about the money, Spider. Maybe it wasn't you who got arrested today, but someday it will be. You need to put that crap behind you. You're an adult now. And you're letting yourself go! I don't recognize you anymore. The drugs and booze have got to stop. Do it for me if you're not going to do it for yourself!"

"I will! I will! It just takes time."

"If you really cared, you would already be sober."

"You can't tell me that I don't fucking care! What the fuck! Only I get to say how I feel! You gonna be a bitch about it?" Helena runs into the bedroom and slams the door shut. "C'mon, baby! I'm sorry. I'm gonna change. It's just hard with all this pressure. I need to do it on my own time. You hear me? I'll cut it out, just give me time. I want this. For you *and* me! C'mon, baby, don't cry. Don't fucking cry again! I'm sorry!"

Harley is barking and running through the hall, tail wagging in an excited confusion. You pound on the door a few more times, but she still does not respond, aside from the gentle whimpers you hear muffled behind the wall.

* * *

Under gray skies, you are staring down at the dead body of a homeless man in the grass at the edge of Harrison Park on 18th Street and Damen just as the EMTs arrive with the fire department to take him away. It is the middle of summer when the drunks spend the mornings to the evenings drinking malt liquor and tequila under the Pink Line tracks, catcalling women with raucous laughter, fighting in the street, and talking shit long past the initial spark of the street lamps at the arrival of dusk.

This man must have died in the middle of the night. Drank himself to death. Alone in the dark. His body is stiff, eyes and mouth open in an expression of shock. Except his right eye looks black. It has been eaten by insects well into the morning. Flies buzz in a halo crowned above his face. He smells like shit and rot. A bottle of Dmitri vodka lies just out of reach from his open hand.

The EMTs brush you out of the way, onto the sidewalk, just in time for you to be honked at by a passing car. A Ford Model A.

"Hey, stranger," Aulina says with a boost of life behind her smile.

"Oh shit!" you call to her. "Long time, no see!"

"What's going on over there?"

"Some guy drank himself to death."

"Lucky!" she laughs. You shake your head. "Hey, get in! Wanna go on an adventure?" You look to her and know that you shouldn't. You know she is bad news, that you two are especially bad news together. You remember how things ended. You remember taking the time to heal from it. You remind yourself of your wife. You are married. You are an adult now.

It is time to grow up and stop being reckless. You remember being an *uliczny opryszek*. A street ruffian. A renegade. But something doesn't feel the same. You don't feel alive anymore. You crave that feeling as much as you crave to be in Aulina's car again, cruising the boulevards like old times. Against your best interest, you jog up to her passenger door and get in.

"Where are we going?" you ask.

"I wanted to stop by St. Adalbert's," she tells you. "I saw it in a dream."

"Is it even open?"

"It doesn't matter, Spider. I dreamt it. I knew you would be here today. Somehow I just knew."

You make small talk while she pulls off to 17th Street and parks in front of the church. Together, you exit the Model A, which shuts off with a pout, and examine the locks on the front entrance. "It's closed," you say. "Anything else you want to do?" But Aulina is hardly listening, she is looking up to the twin steeples. The bell towers stretch into the overbearing gray of the afternoon.

"The scaffolding, Spider."

"Scaffolding?"

"There are ladders on the scaffolding. If we can't get in here, we'll climb to the bell tower!"

"I'm not doing that," you say.

"But you will! I saw it in a dream." Aulina laughs and begins to climb the metal scaffolding up the side of the empty church. You feel you have no choice but to follow her.

"Don't look down!" she calls to you. You do not look down but out. And it is just as bad but twice as beautiful.

You can see all of Pilsen from the scaffolding of St. Adalbert's. You grip the ladder tight as vertigo sets in, taking glimpses of the southwest sprawl of the city, photographing them into your heart with awestruck eyes. Occasionally you slip and fumble as does Aulina. Together you make jabs and awkward jokes to combat the anxiousness. But soon enough you are at the top of the belltower, the smell before rain on the wind. You watch the skyscrapers of downtown from one side as Aulina looks out across her neighborhood from the other.

"We are like kings up here," Aulina tells you. "Untouchable."

"Who does this but you, Aulina?" You laugh. "This is wild. This is fuckin' wild."

Aulina is lighting up a joint, sitting on the edge of the belltower window like there isn't a 10-story drop below her. You run your fingers around the old brass bell of the tower, feeling its roughness, its aged texture, its thickness, its dignified strength. Aulina offers you a puff and you take it and blow smoke out into the open air as the first rain drops fall into the tree-lined streets below.

"Looks like we're stuck here."

"Was this in your dream?" you ask.

"All of it," she says and pulls the joint off your lips for another puff before kissing you. Her touch feels natural. Like turning the pages of an old book. The familiar smell of a library. The right softness. You have rediscovered a past home. And you are in her arms.

While the rain spouts into a torrent, you and Aulina undress each other on the dusted wooden floor of the bell tower and make love in the shelter within the walls of metal scaffolding, only taking breaks to light up and pass between each other until the rumbling of thunder has faded far out across the waters of the lake.

* * *

Your mother is pacing the backyard, looking for four-leaf clovers. Her hands are clasped behind her bent back, head turned down, eyeing the green of the lawn for deviations in the patterns. At her age, this is a process. She moves slow. Her eyes are weak. It is hard for her to bend down into the grass to count the number of leaves. Sometimes this can take her hours.

Your mother has a heart of gold. You have a heart of ice. To your disdain she often calls you a kwiatuszek, *little flower.* Or sometimes she calls you her *szarotka*. But you know she is the mountain flower. Forever the village girl, pure in the depths of her heart. You watch your mother look for the lucky clovers under the gold and black sunset. Cars honk in the street. Birds sail the skies above.

No luck. Tonight, she does not find any. Disappointed, she retires to the kitchen and apologizes. She loves looking for four-leaf clovers whenever it is summer. But the luck is never for herself. Whenever she can find one, she gifts it to you.

* * *

Your wife was serious when she found the photo of you wearing an eyepatch as a child and said she wanted to see where you and your parents once vacationed upon the Atlantic. Now you are walking Harley together down Bayview Avenue, past the Marina, remarking to Helena how things have changed or how fuzzy the memories have become to the point that this town feels foreign to you. You were skeptical to come here. It is like your mother has told you, not to revisit golden memories. *There is always a darkness*, you can still hear her say. And you know this to be true, but you are trying to ignore it for the sake of your wife's experience.

On this trip together, you have fluctuated between intense moments of tenderness and passionate arguments, walking the thin line that can make or break a relationship. Your experience with Aulina has been eating you up inside for months. You are taking your guilt out on her in jabs and petty complaints.

But as you walk south on Bayview Avenue, you are met with a new type of worry. One that shouldn't have to do with your marriage but has webbed out across your lifeline from a specific moment in your youth and spanned across every relationship with a woman you have ever known. You are approaching the fish vendors of the Viking Village. Once when you were young, you fell down here, shoelaces caught in the gears of your bike. A van pulled up to you to help. Faceless girls with cruel intentions. You are shaking. Crying and shaking. You don't wish to walk any further.

"What's wrong with you?" your wife asks. And for the first time in a relationship, a window has opened. A window to the scars of your heart. You have been given a fork in the road. A chance to open up on the realest possible level as to why you are the way you are. Why you do the things you do. You can take it. You can explain everything. She has lobbed you a softball. But you do not swing. Instead, you lash out.

"What do you mean what's wrong with me? I'm just fucking stressed, OK?"

"I've never seen you like this! Your body is shaking, you're sweating. What's going on? Just tell me. Do you need to go to the hospital?"

"I'm all right!" you yell and flail your arms, releasing your grip on Harley's leash before crumpling to the ground. You are crying in the fetal position on a patch of pebbles and sand, wheezing and repeating, "I'm all right! I'm all right! I'm fine! I'm all right! OK?" Harley barks in excitement and nips at your arms and face, and Helena throws her hands up in the air and yells three words that, funny enough, summarize how you feel about the entirety of your life, though this was not entirely her intention.

"What the fuck?"

Heads turn from the fish stalls, and gulls scatter into the air. Harley whimpers in silence and cocks his head as Helena yells again.

"What. The. Fuck?"

* * *

Years have passed. In the factory you have worked your fingers to the bone. The valves have been produced into the thousands. The turn of the wrench is the turn of the hands of the clock, the flipping of the pages of the calendar. The rise and fall of the sun and the moon.

"Back from vacation?" your station mate asks you at lunch. You nod your head.

"Went to a place I've only been at pivotal points in my life. I don't know how to explain it. It's like this place is always calling me. It's like I'm from there, but I'm not. Last day at the beach, I was standing there, and there was this giant fuckin' whale beached on the shore. It was sad and beautiful. I've never seen a creature so big up close. It felt like it meant something, but I don't know what it could mean. So strange ..."

You look to your station mate across the lunch table. He stares at you with blank eyes, unresponsive to your story.

You now notice the earbuds placed inside his ears. He is listening to his music.

At first this disappoints you. But as you chew on your pastrami sandwich and gaze out the window into the gold of the stretching sun, you slip back into the memory. The bloated whale, like a mammoth. A salty fisherman, born on the sea, the last of his kind. The loneliness. The isolation. The spray off the breaking waves and the smell of brine as gulls swoop down at crabs. Brown pelicans dive to fish. You decide you are from there. The ocean. It is just as much your home as the city streets.

* * *

One day to your surprise you receive a call that your mother is in the hospital. Her heart skipped a beat while she leant over to rummage through the grass. You rush to find her in a gurney, hooked up to IV's and beeping monitors, in a white room with overbearing bright lights. She smiles at you when you take her hand in yours, but she is drifting in and out of sleep.

"I love you, Mama," you plead towards her unconscious face, "Kocham cię ... Kocham cię ..."

The doctors take her in for triple bypass surgery. Years of heavy eating have clogged up her heart.

Crying into your palms, you sit alone on a plastic stool in the hospital room considering your mother and the years gone by. The way you never confided in her about your trauma. The way that you took it out on her that you lost your father. You know if you lost her now that you would only take it out on yourself. And then you'd become just like your father. A man you loved and loathed and never understood until now.

Lovers and friends and jobs have all come and gone. They've driven your mind crazy, broken your heart, and swelled your back sore. You never felt you could tell your mother why you and Helena didn't work, never even knew if you wanted it to. Why you always loved Aulina but couldn't create the foundation of a stronger relationship. You couldn't even tell her the buried reasons why you could hardly trust a sexual relationship in the first place. Why you always fought against your own progress. Why you left her alone so much of the time, both living in the closeness of the same city. Why you always lied.

But you *could* have told her. From youth to now the only constant has been the pure heart of your mother. She is the ship that carries you. The North Star that guides it home. She did everything she could because she loved you.

All your life your mother protected you. And when she couldn't, she prayed. You were always on her mind when she wasn't even on yours. Once again you find yourself clenching your hands into fists and rapping them into the sides of your head repeatedly. You are no man. A little boy in a hulking scoundrel's body. Your nerves are a shell barreling through the breakers of a raging sea as pale green as a dollar bill. Bodiless. Too late. It was all a ruse.

You can't bear to face yourself. You want to give up your life. To move on to a holy emptiness. A profound loss of consciousness. One with the ether.

You want to slash your wrists, overdose on pills, walk into traffic and greet the hood of a car or the bumper of a semi-truck with a delirious wide-eyed smile. You want to scream. You want to shout. You want your brains painted on a wall. You want the clockwork days at the factory to come to a sudden end. An aberration of fate. You want to rest. You want to die. But you will not die. Your mother lives. Her love is medicine. You want her to know *your* love *too*.

You decide you will live forever as long as your mother is alive. Maybe Aulina was right. You lived your life one foot in and one foot out. It ruined your marriage. It damaged you and Aulina. It established shallow friendships with no roots to nurture something deeper.

While you wait on news from the doctors, you imagine your future like the montage of a film. The nights will fade by, and the moon will rise and wane in a passing rotation until enough lonely winters pass that you will no longer be a factory stiff. You will be an old man filled with memories gone unspoken. Love left unfulfilled. Then will come the night when you will die peacefully in your sleep, and your soul will ascend above the city of your birth, and you'll look down on Midway Airport and your old neighborhood to see the sky blazing with fireworks in cosmic bursts of reds, greens, purples, and yellows. You will stare at it so long that the city below will shrink into an anthill.

You will get to heaven, and you will slap God across the face with a clap, like an ex-lover, before smiling and drawing in for a deep embrace. God will see you and weep tears of relief that another child has made it home. But you will brush by him. There is someone else there at the gates. A woman that envelops herself around you with her soul.

Your body will glow a celestial white like a szarotka, an edelweiss, a flower that only grows at the dangerous heights of the Alps and Carpathians reaching into the heavens, sought out by romantics willing to risk their lives for material symbolism. Too crazy to be brave.

And where you were an immensely confused scoundrel during life on earth, here you will be good. Your heart will be pure.

You will be forgiven.

AFTERWORD

October is the breath of passing people sifting like spirits in the new-found cold. Just like the smokestacks of the factories along the river coughing out black smog into the gloaming sky.

This old truss bridge has always been here. You walk it in the morning toward the sunrise above the skyscrapers. You walk back west in the evening to the sunset across the inner city. Barges always linger below you, going nowhere. No one is ever visible working on them. Geese and gulls screech and fly off toward the steeples of old Polish churches. You make your way down past the dilapidated restaurants and bars where hipsters and young rich intellectuals carry bags of records, used books, and overpriced vintage clothes, sipping Starbucks and hailing Ubers back to Lakeview and Lincoln Park. You wave through the window to the old man in Zakopane. He barely nods back, slouched over.

The world is not yours.

You ride the 50 bus south, watching the endless upscale glass condos sprout and pop up across the cityscape. They are the blooming of plastic flowers. Weeds clothed in blossomed rose petals, choking out all your memories. The people, places, lovers, enemies, and friends. Almost everything you know.

You make your way to Archer Heights, watching the planes take off from Midway up above your childhood home. You stop at the front and pluck a clover from the grass, then use the spare key to open the door.

Your mother is inside listening to Chopin nocturnes, rummaging through old black and white photo albums of stoic faces from a bygone world. It is hard for her to stand, so you help her. You kiss each other's cheeks and hold one another tight. You hand her the clover, and she smiles.

You close your eyes, recalling a rainy Atlantic day back when you were very young, safe in her arms. Again, you focus on the sensation, the feeling.

To always remember this moment.

ACKNOWLEDGMENTS

A lot of people's support helped make this book possible. I'd first and foremost like to thank Daniel Hoyt and his class at Kansas State University for the effort they put into making this book the best version of itself. I would like to thank my wife, Ayanni,and my family, including my in-laws, for their encouragement to always continue writing. Without the company of my friends, I don't know where I would be. Thanks to Scott Glover, Spencer Baron, Ivo Stoop, K.B., Jack, Jon Garcia, Saul Brambila, Jimmy Garcia, Kyle Eddy, Pete Vercillo, Herb Rosen, Mike O'Connell, all the staff at Delilah's and Liar's Club that I worked with for years, and anyone else I forgot (there are many!) I would like to point out my appreciation to author Patrick Michael Finn for being a guiding voice in the writing world and for providing good literary conversations over the years. Also, thanks to the English Department at Northeastern Illinois University. And a most sincere thanks to Helena at Podhalanka—one tough old lady.

Last but not least: thanks to YOU.